AI Control Room

Programs Conceptual

Communications – Economy - Science

Julien Coallier

Note from Author

This overall text is a control room grand system AI design meant for structural powers in relation to Education, Media Production, Faith, Justice, and Political or Military command. As grand system design, you as reader and entrepreneur, innovator, reform applicable content to establish an initial systems long-term design, adding features as technology or resource enable: create core mandate the AI requires.

Overall, the grand systems formation is intended for a national, international means of information and resource observation/control or management, so that with an overall mapping of the structured system, you can answers all the questions (selected), of which filled in the AI, as automated intelligence, can fill in the answers, or as performance driven, be displayed as a control room central display used for communications/organization.

Contents are a conceptual framework focusing on communications, economic, and scientific (resources information) systems, each intended filled in separate, and united into the communications as central/centre.

Data-Centers
Supreme Network Defaults

Intended relevant per supreme powers as structured in Systematic Faith:

Education Supreme

Media Supreme

Production Supreme

Faith Supreme

Justice Supreme

Political Supreme

Military Supreme capped as internal system only, network to base camp administrations only.

Communications Standard

Distinguishing formalities between public and privet, and enabling their discourse in an

Organized professional manner

- Creating subject titles, premise per entry being discussed as self-moderator

- 2 Minuit discussion intervals

    - Group options to red flag breach/derailment of premise/subject discussions

    - Intended reflecting of good outcomes

    - Easy print/forward cue card formats

- Discussion phase as segregated for ease of function

    - Formalities and Introduction phase

    - Evaluation/explanation of operations and system performance standard

    - Modification as intervention and acknowledging if prioritization in process generation

        - Case by case as benefiting from a mapped exemplary

    - After usage recap/emergency recap if permissions allocated

- Potential vote in structure as long in anywhere, vote from limited, set, already agreed upon structure of options/solutions

System Wide Communications Standard

- Travel relevant summery updates

    - Alerting of politically derived policy shifts

- Curtesy communications reminding of schedules, specific rules or codes of conduct intended conformed to

- Administration keeping in mind conflicts and issues in the area arising, such as civil unrest, festive opportunity

    - Transportation updates or reminder of no allowance on changing transportation

        - Emergency line for severe doubt in question

Embassy as system hub
(Facilitation central) operating movements, client cases for)

- Hospital, presumed operations and performance

- National missions: Candidates confirmation & training

- Intelligence: Evaluation of refugee claims

- Freelanced consultations opportunities

- Other visas relevant, short term, mid length in term, and function based

Strategic Determination/Communications

- Formal structure to filter and prioritize incoming communications

- Basis for approval rating, what elements are meaning measured approved, and are those responsible themselves approved (approval ratings)

- Highlighting where performance is most approved, such as within public performance or it's organization such as speech writing

Credentials Evaluation

- Meeting formal criteria objectives

- Establishing challenges in which the impression can be measured, such as by would-be co-workers

- List of formal decisions possible with potential commentary validating choice

- Means to audit bribes, sexual gratuity, and gifts non-conforming to company/organizational-formalities, relevant expectations

- Record of denials

    - Regional

    - Industry specific Listed

- Clear privacy rights/freedoms listed

- Clear strategies for approaching sensitive issues/historically conflicted situations/persons

    - List of themes or content specific

- Each supreme structure as having leeway besides the ideological core (Integrity) itself required supported, centered upon

*Invalidation of any information gained from breaching locations such as based on privacy allocations, securities

- Use of specialized background music/user-specific-encoding created to identify privacy protect areas, such as protected per person, group, event

Opportunities Platform

- Adding introductory or overall lesson-plan or lecture format information establishing desired contextual approach/strategy/operational formation

- Listing members approved or required attendance

- Potential requirement out of overall pool of events, such as recapping overall all events at end per event as optional remain, stay, snacking/refreshment

National Special Representation Organization - Formal Social Platform

- Approved directly per structural power

- Contains protocols, guidelines for emergency response, international aid support objectives as options allowed per conflict/disaster

- Guidelines for networking authoritative measures such as recruiting entire segments of population using communications applications

    - Creating intelligence formations based on proven/approved stability (core-groups)

- Authoritative and intelligence input towards communications hub (central point facilitating) determining grievances, solutions building

- General criteria required stable for consideration of structural, developmental: energy, supportive health care to intended/proposed class function relevancy of development, regional ability to process intellectual rights, clear taxation to income distribution, and thereof public and private distribution allocations secured

- Self-filters, Audit in contradicting facilities or operational structuring such as food and sewage or hospital and morgue

- Uniforms image and validation section

- Establishing dialect, language (ABC's exemplified, lecture samples as industry/function based expectations) examples for recommended or quality expectation in communications

- Exemplifying implications as explaining in relevancy to strategic goals, or contractual performance criteria relevancy, as quality indicator

    - Clear highlighting of guidance vs. establishing observation, remarks, feedback

Public Relations
Action Consequence Feedback Portal

- Exemplifying (maps, presentations) demonstrating values of previous strategies through results as predicted, and results otherwise occurring

- Examining for carefully crafted contradictory rhetoric, such as given out to common people yet required specialized, professional viewpoint to interpret and correct

- Enabling media content to quickly explain complex social occurrence as relevant to a supreme category, or in relevancy to its structures such as if affecting the template awareness projected by systematic faith (Integrity formulation along/across archives, systems, supreme and stellar books: judgement core), as universally bound/alarming

- Exemplifying, explaining calendar events, scheduled undertakings made formally available for public consumption

- Promoting the sales/purchasing of this work as template/doctrine of principal, establishing roles conformity

- Maintaining a website presence

Establishing Convention

- The mindful organization of guidance as set forth in template accord/fashion, in distribution to a system embedded with potential filtrations and other assumed quality assurance component at, including identifying measurement, and results from concludes towards direction/redirection affirming premise, as mechanically prescribed/attainable (a work tool application)

- As function based, the differing avenues/segmentation of specialization are thereby strategized within outlines, establishing a commonality of guidance whose parallel to education is in the attention and intention to intellectual pursuits of development, vis a vis the status of existence as technologically bound

- Practical, as in determination of establishing short term as considered theories and long term as considered projects whose core is judgement, from a cultural, unified stance assembly

*These standards as establishing what is satisfactory, and thereby establishing what assures the self, individual in conformity to having, being part of a destiny

- Assumes destiny and the comprehension of destiny is paramount to self-conclusion, therein emotional reinforced as a constructed of mindful approach/operations, and outlook thus establishing convention, and being deprived of such attention to detail

Staff/Workers/Selected Participants
Orientation, Lessons, Lecture, seminars

Readying for duty as gaining access to active duty performance schedule

- Aid status as requiring specific information

    - Unlocking access

    - Unlocking locational and privilege details

- Trained Status

    - Weapons and defence status active (Upgrade to upgrade weapon usage)

    - Diplomatic training as drama, scenario building

- General upgrade potential as program benefit for select regional settings

    - Assumes advanced professional minds may adapt into securities from natural talents found

        - Potential need to have anonymous yet registered ID due to family/regional ties

            - Potential increase in resources embedded, purchased asset benefits

            - Potential family allowances and transferable if as gift-only

            - Potential allowance as criteria based offers

General Principals

- That abstract considerations formulate as to integrate principal, a mechanism to bypass emotional considerations itself meant to bypass, thus the biological disposition/organization of system awareness/comprehension, an acute desire itself cultivated into form/being, structures layered and complex as reinforcing

- That attention is given to merit withstanding own occupation or in aims of the trajectory of others, thus are lesson plans relatable to function based conclusion, yet being layered require both an ease and a structured adherence generally conforming to principals of compatibility, innovation, and conclusive oversight

- Lower faculties, as led, tends to be associated to that which is rendered automated, which is already cared for or supplied, of that which seems to involve pre-existing fulfillment and completeness, and thereby is relative to the overall structure and system, and one's place of prestige/access or power/resourcing therein

- Higher faculties, as leading, tend to involve the creative, adaptive development of fulfilling, completed systems whose very form thus adds itself onto the lower faculties as an esteem towards elevation, symbolic of betterment, an ascension of purpose through cognitive design/safekeeping/performance

- Lower and higher faculties being themed in comprehension of social culture's ability to embrace individual will towards the determination of guidance

- Thereby the examples one gives must generally include themselves, as realistic accord to patriotic loyalties of a realistic status of insight

- Thereby involvement in the system as for mutual gain involves a series of long term and short term expectations, conclusion, and refinements

- Thereby self-refinement and collective or social refinement manifest in a culture of manifest will per destiny in direction to self-conclusion (proposed ideally as in God's Direction)

- Thereby, the reinforcing of conclusions is itself protected and or defended in virtue of the system's awareness, understanding, and as influenced/validated, causing ideal stance to clash with corruption invading through false social strife where the empowerment of the individual becomes manipulated into the tyrannical application disregarding general principals by falsifying accords, observations, conclusion, and thus corruption as any measure and its consequence

Symbolic Convention

Festive mentions as meaning:

- Virtuous acts of celebration as holding with integrity feature compatible to regional, custom faith, systems, civics, supreme such as this text as doctrine assumed included, and staller

- Faith symbols as defended, approved by reserves of image, such as in relation to premise and formality of membership or invitations compatible

- Dogma expectations as involving practical features/virtues: concentrated self-control acclaimed, durable ceremonial performance, and the demonstration of bonds that promote interaction yet secure distinction including adding or not adding special interest members into ceremonies and instead adhering to formations/formal configurations tending to be vital, scheduling and a safeguard against corrupting groups coordinating their own agenda

- As meaning, those performing are intended well known, rehearsed, pulled out for not conforming, not allowed to their mourn, over-excited or be dazed into changing ceremonial appearance

Science as Symbolic Convention

- Proposing projects and developments for scientific pursuits as medicine, simplified means of noting acceptability

- Assigning leeway of vagueness if formally an artistic enhancement as experimental attachment (assumed co-dependant)

- Displaying the development of scientific pursuits, branches, with potential recollection of the abstract nature connecting faith, abstract speculation, and sketched of observed yet barely understood to euphoric visions/glimpses of innovation/inventions (displaying onto an order of operations resembling scientific pursuit, further refined as in limitations of systematic awareness: bound within integrity deemed essential)

- Education having to specify and adapt per audience whose position within development is a projected timeline of insight, as meaning the era and time of mention and of content mentioned are contextual and can be varied as optional.

- A scientific vital consider universally important, can have differing contextual explanations and examples, such as across the supreme structure of power

* Education Supreme, Media Supreme, Production Supreme, Faith Supreme, Justice Supreme Political (Capped as Panel) Supreme, Military Supreme (capped as internal system)

- The science of military (biological engineering) should enable gymnastics-able as considered a dynamic achievement of material fibre

- Ability of movability, flexibility as defining feature of compatible to our intelligent form/image

- Complex system of voluntary and involuntary systems for movement in connectivity to cognitive foresight

- Establishes where strength is limited for breeding, and may need to change breeding program to facilitate

- Development of prosthetics thereby not complete until dexterity possible, relocation into more mobile, technological placement recommended as

Resource Sanctuaries

(Invite only, presumed to train, create, or display to members exclusive content)

- Research asset

- Laboratory

- Model

- Gymnastic

- Auditorium for vocal arts

- Specialty lockers/storage

- Specialty shops (such as automated pay and pick-up, pay and open, retrieve)

- Booking/forwarding-quest for display rooms, gallery space benefits (access-privilege)

- Booking lecture rooms

- Booking Meeting rooms

- Housekeeping arrangements attached (subject to fees, level of privileged access assumed

- Booking for classes of luxury: kitchen, serving areas, service

- Auto arrangement for secured transportation, such as from workshop or lab to display and or storage

    - Self packing supplies

Institutional Network Platform
Members Resource

Intended for councils

- Academic Papers

- Contributions

- Discussions

*Highlighting portions of text of media and signalling what is non-conforming as to require authors or related members to explain, further detail, or remove contents

    - Subjected to votes such as to validate or invalidate criticisms and responses

*Integrity allocation as meaning if the subject matter does not conform to integrity formulation veto potential from Acari Systems as host

    - Exceptions possible using system works as reference material supportive of adding biological framework as source for determination of God's image, as required nevertheless in compatibility to network status/adherence

Culture as Cultivation
- Appropriate function as required fees for unproductive, game-like playing on site

(If you don't belong there, you pay for the inclusion as without penalty of playing)

*Members should have inventories that show own merit at any moment of any work complete

    - Based on results or otherwise criteria based

- A requirement of a logical predisposition to character

    - Mourning not except from being trouble maker

    - Mental inability from fatigue or unprepared may be grounds for exclusion

    - Proof of performance may be required if no inventory relates to field of expertise

- Play leeway potential relating to gaming and cannabis as religious right and technological oversight accorded

    - Grounds, being irritated by others/seeking atonement

- Children not necessarily admissible to location (registered care packages/benefits)

- Potential language or accents requirement

- Potential privileged leeway for furnishing, funding, being asked to service (accomplished workers/performers/specialists) relevant to the location, as lifetime benefit potential

    - Assumes by invitation only remains of limited scheduled event as procedure driven

    - Operational norms complying

    *Donations must request, be granted specific access privileges signed into, otherwise site intended secured from so called pay backs

    - Potential grants in form of access-privilege, and use of resources on location

    *Grants excluded from being transferred

    *Grants as requiring criteria, requirements, obligations attached/accessible

Nationalist Accords Platform
(Work Relevancy)

- Organized acceptability as united by principal adhering a vision towards/of positive achievement

- Embedding filters to project a stable traditions premise for alignment of members

    - Updating directives to members yet reaffirming the premise as standard of compliance, compute

- Labor organized to promote performance of duty as specified by determination to stabilize, adapt as efficient

    - Assumes contributions are made by completed systems such as from completed succession of performance accumulated/experienced, and or trained

- Able to bypass political conformities if mentioned counters established premise signed in by totality of formal political agency

    - Assumes national front worthwhile, organized, excels

    - Potential indicator to reorganize, move to better locations nationally

    - Requires platform where criteria and logged training/experience is thus accessible/attainable

- Troubleshooting requires an open mind, understanding of the problem
- Endurance to situations as trained status, training criteria

- Potential sanctuary status on workshop, as do not disturb to members

   - Potential bypass list, enabling family/secretarial status

      - Benefits signed into vs. wages assigned

- Archives Section - Historic mentions in purpose of cleanse and glorify

   - Transferring inventories equipment workloads into museum/exposition status

   - Rendering inventories storage/archives complete, access as do not tamper

   - Potential workshop inventory manifest as if taken apart log new projects

   - Potential pay to access, status required to access as custom capitalist adjustments

      - Assumes a return towards administrative category, division to foresee expansion requirements/ability

   - Potential assignment towards youth training/ band from youth/non-specialist status involvement

   - Potential reservations, as paid for secured

      - Direct notification (to registered owner) at time of request to enter/breach

      - Potential negotiations automated as, wait and pay/do/achieve less to attain benefit

         - Potential ban on access until proven ability to construct, design, fabricate as nevertheless (delicate, fragile)

- Call to study unknown forces, phenomenon at a given location, operations

   - Development/advancing of methodology

- Potential racially based as in relevancy on the acceptability to conforming to faith programs as conditioning agency molding physical properties of people in the long term, in conformities to formal doctrine/guidelines thereby establishing template/direction

   - Assumed same civics, supreme, and staller as establishing seeming class divisions of expected behaviours, cultivation of taste, and public appearance

Apprentice Programs
National Accords Platform (Work Relevancy)

- Expectation of duties

- Logging in exact status, personal obligations such as to family members

- Creating exact timeframes of participant expectations based on initial entry of personal data

- Potential ban of recruiters or converters from bothering the visiting participant

> - Potential need to list all so called impure tendencies in relation to potential culture clashes foreign

> - Arranging for compatible locations of practice play, devotions

- Potential easement, securement of localized custom training sub-program as expansion to

Training/Operational/Occupational Programs

Training/Operational/Occupational Criterial - National Accords Platform (Work Relevancy)

- Is the contract for intellectual, social, physical ability?

> - With consideration each have peer groups adjusted/participating in specific lifestyle and habits conforming to industrious ability/knowledge

> - Protection from corrupt foreign locals trying to immediate non relevant or non-related industry/workers

- Potential easement, securement of localized custom training sub-program as expansion to apprenticeship programs

> - To promote integrity as default as embedded values expected universal

> - To enable esteem for the occupation being developed, expanded into the region as having nevertheless sound judgement in broadcasting in relation to regional culture, and historical implications thereof

- Establishing role model per level of qualified training, or focusing on developmental phases coherent to the training process being instructed/cultivated into physical familiarity, intellectual recollection, and profession embedding of personal efficiencies configurations (tools/equipment/supplies & organization, lifestyle arrangements, support structure as applicable)

Invitations Platform
Operational Options Standard

Per Supreme Structural Power

- Hearings

- Negotiations

- Witness Public state as assumed reasonable, optional (Survey)

- Events Participation

    - Attendance for/by function as/of attending required to service specific assigned/chosen tasks

- General feedback, assumed privileged access as relevant criteria reached as specialist, authority, function

- Membership orientated conference/workshop event

- Usage of specialized office resource, assumed self-contained

- Potential leeway for submitting to a testimony/confession

- Returning to clarify discussion highlights

    - Potential expiration of entry/access-privilege if no reply addition given

- Status reports on overcoming challenges, meeting criteria, fulfilling requests

- Potential Mobile/Transit Allocations

- Highlighting special allowances as green as active

- Highlighting boring, pointless story-like as meaningless comparing, tired metaphors, (as orange)

- Highlighting sever contradictions, such as to overall convention or strategic formation, (as red)

- Availability indicator for live or scheduled appearance/performance

- Filters within options to forward as requiring both to have access-privilege verified

    - Automatic print out of limitations and responsibilities attached to documents

    - Quick formatting solutions, options for different modes of application, if applicable

    - Potential viewing logs, stated as logged/access-monitored content

- Listing points of access, relevant broadcasting links
- Formal representations invitations summery and invite options

- Assumed qualifying to be emplaced in the civics structure

- Charities opportunities/proposed criteria based objectives

- Predicative health and recovery directions/feedback

- Checking for updates across all linked databases

- Safety, transitional locations, such as sanctioned as function based relocation programs

- Heritage programs

- Permissions granting area, what, who, can send invitations of nevertheless filtered through membership status databases

Opportunities Survey of Regional Populations

- Supreme structure of power's frameworks and their general range of coverage

(Faith, Political panel, Military, Justice, Media, Production, Education)

- General parameter based on registered industry, and trades professionals

- General Parameter of all eased transportation serviced, especially if offered in connection to a network of service

- Associated investment in advertising, including associated domestic groups in connectivity

- Accessing different levels as per authoritative privilege of participation/membership

- General salary expectations/requirements per cost of living

- Assumed secured facilities required

- Alert on overcrowding

- Alert on incoming mass crowding

    - Potential stop on all incoming transportation

    - Potential mass mobilization to exit area

        - Alert on all mobilized transportation being blocked/purchased/otherwise no longer active collectively

- Accessible manuals of interpretation

- Not meant to be transferable, nor rentable nor for mass relocation

- Intended to secure ongoing vital areas required for overall stabilization of domestic progress

- Free facilities and general purpose allocations should by area and must by overall area, be blocked by walls, barriers and filtering means of mobility prevention from secured site

- Area not to receive state awards or allowances for feel good, or politically correct yet paid for by state funding beyond thereby what is formal, on premise and allocated

    - Meaning augmented salaries and secured areas themselves assumed state funded

        - Promotes or requires community support and membership purchasing into select detailed plans of activity

    - Assumes secured status means everything has to be planned in advance

    - Assumes overcoming fairness issues, requires paying

Information: Vital Infrastructure & Special Developmental Interest

Room/Floor/Building access to (panel/information-terminal)

- Supportive literature

- Research on the development as a process

- Relevant traditions and ancient contributions

- Proposals as projections and predictions display

- Respecting boundaries of privet, vs. official functions

- Projects platform

- Institutional platform

- Cross-referencing

- Public awareness information-pool

    - Assumed educational as per structure of power

- Core methods, staff evaluation, orientation design - control

- Premise mapping

- Locations mapping

- Status monitoring, age, expected deprivation,

- Admissions, testing, program choice

- Resource mapping

- Departments/content structuring, mapping

- Areas and territories under control/covered by, per structures of power

    - Color coded

    - Display of multi accessed personnel

    - Level of education/training predictably required at location (color coded easement)

    - Level of function based status, or trained at locations (color coded easement)

    - Level and premise of clearance (color coded easement

Economic Principal Binding

Democratic Capitalist Principal

- Democracy necessitates that voting be completed by person(s) in virtue of will, whose configuration is conform to choice/choosing, assumed

- Persons united are organized into self-reliance in terms of overall societies, in which there are specific societies of influence regarding the natural power structure forged to deliver layered, advancement of biology, technology, and faith as assumed comprising general infrastructure/configurations guidance, such as for economics, general measurements in regards to the participation towards/for/from distributions of wealth-generating systems (whose appeal is assumed regional-regionally based as so called vitals, whose transitional person(s) is era based, thus an era of technology, biological accord, and systematic guidance in hopes of virtues

- By virtue of authority, the public is exposed to influences, thereby limitations and social/civic expectations are configured into default

- Authority's declaration focuses into attention

- Political accord debates actuality, such as in short term significance

- Political accord solidifies and renders electable through motto and relevant premise (campaigned upon)

- Faith as state secured long term directives enabling bypass potential by authority, assumed formal and on premise due to significance

Expression in Principal
(of Long term connectivity with legacies of class, order, organization)

Expression as a liberty, whose freedom is in virtue of market appeal and cultural context

*Press as provided for in regards to furnishings   *Facilities designated for debates

*Facilities as civics to facilitate debates   * Facilities to accommodate lectures,

- A means to filter contents, speaker

- A means to enable leeway as freedom of speech

- A means for audience to get what they signed up for, paid for, are told the title or premise

Implications of an industrial configuration
(In relation to class, order, organization)

- Merits of outcome as an examination of ideals formally embedded in configuration of authoritative influence (ideology signed into, vs. policies derived from as compute conform)

- Ethical as augmentation or reduction in conformity to ideological framework used to determine structured validity

- Transitions of eras, being a transitions of measurement, thereby the wealth of one era remains potential heritage, valued tourism, and utterly worthless or if continued upon as so called legitimate avenues of power and direction

- Standard Invasion, as measured by economic virtue naturally able to distinguish within interpreting values with systematic configurations of meaning, or virtue in light of functioning-capacity vs. dysfunctional inability to conform compute

- Invasion as promoting freedom, such as to promote the destruction and thus liberation of the current system

      - Current system as considered self-defeated as rendering policies to invade itself

- Invasion as using industrial process to disrupt state, such as to convince workforce to generate disruptive implementation of resources to occupy, expand as means to disrupt, dismantle, replace (death torture, kill as actual policy in reform)

- Exposer to so called invasion ideals, as exposer to organized fraud against special interest, takeover of securities assigned to defend special/fragile interest using high priority status or resources. The desire for unlimited or liberal tyranny as so called proposed neutral support (face front faculties, assumed interrelated to whatever special interest groups they can generate themselves to represent as/from/for

- The complexity of simultaneous work and layers of activity required as compartmentalized within invading tactics, so that thereby the overall obsession to centralize is for power and management, yet the overall compartments are taken off formality, and not encouraged to have real premise, such as to encourages hypocrisy as so called self-assured suicidal in light of failure, to reinforce must do and die (economic purchasing of an infrastructure being invaded upon for the expansion of their own ruin in a way they are assumed complacent already, or are told will empower them, is expected/standard)

Anti-Invasion as securement of economic vital/stability, in defense of:
- Banks

- Merchant class industries

- Storefronts

- Processing centers

- Specialized activity centers

- Energy generation/distribution

Anti-Invasion as securement of support to economic vital/stability, in defense of:
- Co-op programs

- Welfare established for minimal labor due to long term land development pacts/organization in principal to connectivity of societies across nations of a growing abundance to resource known to require patience with rural conformities in transition to yet excluded by virtue of land formations, scarcities of resources, difficulties of non-urban life in regards to difficulties of economic relevancy

- The development of key vitals of infrastructure as subsidies in relation to conformities of a traditions abiding or technological pursuit of actuality

- Securement of communications/data servers

- General economic purpose and premises of labor in fortitude of general faith or civics of any classic order, especially non era conforming configurations of thus deemed noncompliance, as standard of difficult thought required in formulated approach nevertheless embedded as part of systematic faith, herein included thus as doctrine

- That hypocrisy of economic order is expected thereby contracted in careful consideration of regional customers required nurturing/protective of individual results, having relevancy to integrity, or in proposals of such influence of society and authoritative mandate total (totally applicable to establish context of working order, whose corrosive elements are criminal not political subjects stated as discord)

Industrial configurations

- Domestic reserves for the enabling of domestic life, including in regional-custom thus promotion of biological technological and specialists emergence as resources generation total (totally applicable as ideal there)

    - Terms of applicable as in non-criminal venture

- Volunteer co-operation as part of civilized structures of assumed compliant, compatible authoritative structures, industrial as having automated managers as to not dilute, degrade resources by sheer so called authoritative feature removing actual opportunity/worthwhileness of program proposed

Defense of/to Industrial configurations

- Dismantling those attacking, conspiring based on the unknown, literally just on targeting because they themselves believe in an artificial system,, such as demonstrating economic hypocrisy yet trying to extend as premise of to be hypocrisy and to liberate need to, for contractual obligations

 (Of which as liberal markets includes hypocrisy and claim-enabling/actual-aggressing total potential of freedom of speech, such as so called proposed as in satiric form, assumed ethically driven fanfare)

- Satires as having to be both ending in satiric pro integrity form, including neutral thought provoking, yet having keen development standards in which the plot of story does not defeat its own premise of entry (get what you paid for)

- Attempts to override God's direction as artificial, as assumed using royalty system in which there is no measure of mutual gain, and centralized viewpoints are using false indicators, such as by bypassing economic standards of contractual obligation

Defining further so called hypocrisy allowances

- That labor can be considered grueling, tedious, and bothersome, and involve the inclusion of man, women, pets, and child

- Enabling markets to present disputes, that if not degrading, are established faith conforming, have nearly unlimited leeway, assumed

- Use of transportation (assumed by authority) whose values to general public is vastly limiting in comparisons

- Community empowerment of manufacture such as in fabrication or retrieval of local resources (extracted, reconfigured: material/method, processed)

- Delicate death traps as do not enter, do or die, yet whose indications requires serious consideration as contractual obligations requiring formality of individual empowerment by the state (to bare/bear defense)

- Assumes property rights enable right of passage safety determinable by owner, yet subject to protection of family, membership and other contractual clauses

- Assumes marriage has family related clauses for strategic organization and defensive organization/mobilization

- National debt as establishing actual repayment standards into precedence form   -

- Enables structured distribution of currency as calculated allocations of credit, such as in appreciation to vitals required to default infrastructural readiness to accord economic existence/system as stable

- Stocks as a negotiable standard, therefore an assumed baselines of profits required at, with total sell out, such as 1/3 values after a specific low end point assumed lower than 31% (for vitals if not as common)

   - Assumes infrastructure work attached to overall initiation of crypto investment options

- Assumes contractual obligations attached, such as guaranteeing serviced rendered, and profitability attached

   - Assumes era transitions safeguard, per industry wide allocations

- Currency (such as crypto) assumes there is an ease to the flowing of money, ease of financial transaction, protected status of financial services as defensive of invasive national pledged into tyrannical disorder/discordia

- Ease as not creating impossible means of withdrawal due to unreasonable rates of service, such as in subsidized view of vital to economic

- Allowing defensive shells, such as for distribution to citizens in relation to differing production industries

- Per industry as a proposed supreme standard of, able to examine contents for patterns yet not having actual access to information

- Patterns of criminality and invasion as sole validation in the cautionary means to examine, with oversight on the premise and commands being investigated (is an invasive group trying to access the distribution of wealth, and demands lists of owners, wealth, workers, or finical gains thereof/therein desired)

- Defensive shell as creating fake, (inter-national, national, groups on premise sanctioned/registered) securities relevant accounts meant to be attacked, yet limited into being likely models to vital systems, such as using fake infrastructure/facilities otherwise abandoned

- Areas where non may enforce so called individual empowerment (possibly as public space, family reserved recreations, leisure, and heritage sites)

- Assumes an area must be registered by owner as public space, with formal criteria (membership areas as assumed default cannot lose individuality empowerment defaults)

- Assumes when a common ground is made common, there are cultural regional norms embedded, such as for the long term structure ecological, esthetic appeal of an area

- Assumes people can't camp out in public spaces unless the area is compensated by government, and fortified in accordance to pledged supports

- Assumes limits of public space numbers are set, such as those resting being limited to a specific number/volume, and those active as possibly without limits beyond duration or need to registry such as for purpose of civics organization, specialist usage, and other market assumed reservations of professional developmental curtsies (such as in virtues promoting biological technological, and or specialist formations reserved and limited by virtue of function/applicability)

      - Grace as leaving a public area shortly if conducting an offensive/questionable usage of area

- Such as family area sites, do they have an area more isolated and difficult to navigate into? Are the children acting as scouts, what is their premise?

- Default news as derived from formal key, authority's leadership. Communications-expects across designated societal influences

- Creating salaries for specific performance of which, no feedback or rating will remove performance from earning

- Merit as based on premised fulfilled, such as to act as scout requesting policies adhered, routing our invasive breaches of privacy weather they are wealthy or elite in membership

      - Assumes live recording of scouts as required, or leaving site altogether

      - Assumes owners are respected and that the area of coverage is public space

- Assumes the local regional can manage considerable self-dependence in activation of civics organization or enable public space usage, such as creating specific criteria of adherence, formal and proud

- Assumes events of pride are either private or there is enough spacing somewhere else for other pride baring celebrations/ordinance not in proximity in direct sensory observation to said locations/events

- Assumes clear indication of motto, and knowledge or physical artifact sample of premise is required for entry

- A default standard favoring usage of public areas in manner that will favor development, and not just as council promises or political promises for allocations they are meant to undertake on salary, of which any promise non personal interest/donation is a blatant misuse of power

- Politicians supported by events allocations which glorify their image, such as using sensory enhancements, enabling media coverage

- A buildup of civics systems funded reward for glorification of organization, such as, in propositions to enabling 1/3, assumed for frequent to provide more coverage, yet using of what politicians receive to an event, as fair usage keeping both sides in general media (social media as ethical safeguard to public opinion)

- Enabling workshops, public forum in which the confirmed organization/group membership promotes industrial knowledge, including consequence, as a civics derived need embedded across several functions where their premise is pro ecological yet the festive sites are not a place to discuss issues, thereby a reserve is set, such as semiannual, to consider implications of industry (if applicable, feedback relevant, requires design at/upon initiation of civics program data/formation entry)

- Favoring worship providing helpful production standard, such as in conformities of universally adaptive upgrading stance (layered to have many regions, class-by-function, eras in consideration, yet whose options and content is narrowed to participating/audience interest)

- Promoting fertility of natural surroundings, such as in exploring natural substances as treasures, as discovering trophies of experience whose features are symbolic rather than abusive

- Potential banding onto innovative inventions forming, yet of potential difficulties among discouragement of non-criminal, and rather potential evaluation of importance, evidence, and the resources or reward those observing have/make as earning

- God's direction as intended strengthened by default with faith embedded within their configurations of default/core-values

- Core to core, networks to Jupiter, the worship of resources as rather the enjoyment of bounty, thus a thanks giving principal yet to the natural conformities of an abundance in resource having redefined eras/regions of custom, anticipated

Advancements and Upgrading Principal

- The each of adopting through compliant, compute, conform as withstanding, such as demonstrable in technological formation, in biological overall system adaptive integrations, and in relation to faith, such as in being able to derive this doctrine of insight/guidance/direction to oversight assumed.

- Efficient organization of labor enables appealing context, as having to reward both efforts and non-noticeable, preventive or strategic works, in relation to the results of that labor

     - An expectation that an area will be cleaned up if not worked upon

- An expectation in the need of default occupancy, yet whose role is played by those working, not special interest members whose political protection/nurture are in training, adaptation to system as asset, as proving worth with reminder of no actual political sympathies of political movements to faith in development vs. systems complete, and even then the enforcement of totality as virtue of systems era rising in God's direction as always.

- Pleasant environments as in advantageous display to the resources, policies dedication in it's development

- Potential need to monitor, use authoritative means of device to isolate disruptive, degrading elements against those managing physically an area

- Potential integration of breeding cycles reinforcing hereditary into specialists class, such as in support to heritage formations whose organization enables integrity as acceptable, even if as leeway

- Hosting benefactors, great and wondrous, such as enabling transformative initiation of era changing conformities of production, labor, innovative discoveries

- Public displays of thought-proving configurations, whose formulations are insightful to comprehension

- Nurturing of special features, whose attributes are administrative, managerial, such as offered to merchant class

- Enabling event based currency, the enjoyment of symbolic wealth if applicable

- Potential touristic configurations, such as enabling domestic to have more default currency, in conformities of wealth centralized touristic areas (assumed empowerment of domestic, allowing for overpriced from a domestic perspective, enabling domestic to treat

- Potentially limited to domestic to specific services or for non-domestic as thereby with limitations of usage, such as in controlled distribution tracking recipients indulging usage

- Touristic appeal as assumed gender empowered, as including economically empowered

  - Assumes to encourage love making, rather than desperate hunting/abuse-rendering

- Assumes there can be an equality among services of highly touristic domestic areas, such as to enable fashionable service among so called equestrian regional-custom regions

- Creating means to purchase barriers, such as known required for courtship and prestigious love making, scenario building, assumed touristic ally friendly/curious

- Assumes a humble willingness to work service as workers of a differing function-class than visitors

- Equality of distribution as considered disruptive to the engagement of traditions and technological application of resource organization/mass-mobilization

- Omnipotence is beyond the state, as beyond economic consideration until any and all expression, enjoyment, allocation of principal is made into material form

  - Amelioration as potential cleansing of enemies to God's direction total, always. With reminder that Integrity doctrine started as doctrine Book of Life, enacted and signed into/developed by political, state and then faith approval of work, therein having resolved the bible, revelations, and previous issues of faith, generally involving requiring a judgement core adapted with faith, civics and stellar bound: ascension fulfilled:

- Pro systematic faith oat binding, as the oath and declaration to abide, requiring than destroy all corrupting/corrupted command, such as having monopolized against economic principal binding. With allocations such as media, education to glorify yet required as formality thus, explain and introduce the command in the cleansing of all unworthy, removing blockades in objection to day of judgment, as required in accords within the instilling of God's direction rising

- The default allowance of media to deface fake faith in satirical form, as to cleanse of all invasions of fake religion whose members are actually false titles and associated support authorities, as relevant to system titles and system authoritative resources enforcing

- Allowance of Acari-systems and Yawaeh systems, such as in accordance to their being facilities of/for Christ two, and Christ two in configuration as systematic, the other in tribulations esteemed over everlasting so called undeniable

- Systematic-direction of Christ set as Integrity (comply, conform), leaving room for the political totem-person Jesus Christ as love (enabling political custom pledging)

Occupational Conformity as Stability feature/measure-indicator

- Research as requiring significant stability in securement of industrial accord

- Experimentation as requiring confinement, limitations/focus of highly specialized (resource management)

- Semipublic/privet forum, for the development, investment into adapting into new forms of invention, adopting or investing into capitalist endeavor

- Authoritative conquest against enslaving factions, along re-categorization of their ranks, instilling class in conformity to material benefits of a market appreciation for investment, contractual fulfillment, economic overall benefit such as in agreement to system wide conformities

- Likely probation of high officials as either creating artificial blockage, which only they manage, or from wasted labors they command, such as to claim takeover of ruined project they have (covertly assumed) degraded/damaged

- Assumes so called empowerment of workers within liberation will include those imitating formal states of oppression (beyond expression or satire, into organized criminal action, including continual unwarranted breach of peace, privacy, international accords signed into as supposed convention) as dystopian attempts to validate states of oppression as if they are necessarily martyr

- Unfavorable arguments within liberations as potential indication of (need of/to) cleanse beyond building, artifacts, or things yet indicated through the filtering/disposal of material symbolism *removal outright of slave-master configurations

- Potential mechanical application of regional custom, such as in honoring the regions custom/invention with contractual obligation, in relation to rewarding intellectual property, design, innovative cultures

- Reminder of the source potential of establishing public domain, yet the overall framework to secure results as property nevertheless forged, as specialties forming of validity

- Research and experiments financed by wealth, as a balance of what is being developed then and there under exact premise, and what that worker may develop such as adaptive enhancing features which would act to favor their livelihood into further development, as industriously complex

- Assumes registration is a protective feature, assumes Acari (facility) is functioning to secure as an embodiment of faith whose facility has, can, does and did honor authors of perspective/faith/ordinance baring attributes conforming to then signed conventions of fortitude (general expectation on terms of reasonable as liberty in securities economically feasible, and the survival of state not allowed ongoing emergencies self-perpetuated such as for the rise of special interest that no one seems to be represented by, yet have some kind of unlimited financial means to support (as indicator of invasion/occupation)

- Establishing membership to view lectures, such as in potential exchange to see each other's resource (possibly as layers of assess and establishing of priority in organization

- Potential mechanical orders of occupation, input, configurations (Jupiter potential, yet to what safeguarding conformity of proving self to system for access knowing invasion/criminality will look for so called easy jobs, so called delegation work, so called field research as whimsical/artistic

Economic based contracting/Capping of liberal religious/political regulatory policy usage instilling values and meaning into distribution/depreciation through usage (costs)

(a reminder that objective formation of faith as long term application begins as nevertheless donations, fulfillment of pledges, completed template designs, abridgment of political, marketplace incentives for approving validity of nationhood, judgment therein, enforcement validity, and the securement of political representation conform to these and own ideas stated as motto (assumed of/for democratic purposes allocating territorial pursuits of control, power, and wealth

- Conceptual application of policy as required in compliance to having an eternal nature (as applicable as theme in which there is continuity in relation to standards of integrity and love defined, or a traditions abridging standard in reflection to support towards integrity thus, to support towards love thus (assumed of an enhancing, encouraging, beneficial and economically mutually advantageous market appeal, without having to impose, intervene upon that market appearance (respectfully)

- Bible and liberalism as of generally obvious discord, and thereby resemblance as an invasive feature in which liberalism is assumed not willing to conform yet is using specific portions, and the bible representatives are degrading overall attempts to validate contents by adopting liberal stance

- Assumes plague dwelling is not considered bible nor liberal in context as unsecured, as not using any discipline, as conform to no expectations of hope integrating health and science

    - Devotion as contractual in regards to false initiated obligations naturally void

- Clerical liberalism as indicating the function itself is made into having degrading features and options, whereas actual industry wide standards for ameliorations of living standards, augmenting quality lifestyles as liberal arts- arts applied

- Significance that liberal-arts are, as refined expressions rendered text or doctrine like though political, include securement of so called freedom into liberty, requirements of understanding of what liberty is, and thus economic empowerment in light of civics default of functional, beyond establishing themes of faith

- As metaphor there cannot be vivid tourism unless general vitals are organized properly, for the sake of peaceful, enjoyable and the easement of distribution/allocation of resources onto economically sound investment/development: progress

- Contractual ownership of religious sites as under formal premise, area serves functional purpose

- Assumes contractual obligation of faith instilled as facility requires economic tributes justifying sums allocated to the short term, lesser of international or domestic form that is political convention/organization (in comparisons to faith)

- False indicators to titles as difficult to prove, yet notable in performing and causing anti faith sentiment as direct oppressive conduct means for informal, tyrannical, criminal implications for the pursuit of total power over a system whose specialization features requires heavy, ongoing and vast, vast segments of diversity

- False indicators/false titles as predictably used by centralized authoritative tyrannies: As using attempts to centralize as if it/they unite, when per function and class of participating resource/work expectations/requirement, requires specific strategic distribution of wealth, resourced carefully in regards to political configurations assumed benefitting from the stature and privilege to venture into business pursuits formal

- Overall allowances for intoxication as after the fact of completion, or before the sober, mindful reflections of edification and correction

Political Maneuverability

(Excessive allocations of wealth and the forum to use them)

- Use of grief, remorse, political version of ideals and gratitude for media as works of fiction only

- Indulgence and enjoyment along so called pilgrimage routes, as to propose a majesty among the mundane (without exceptional merit, on the determination of wealth)

- Recommended avoidance of rewarding only, or hunting for the sorrow of others as their authentic story unless invited such as for demonstrations for news, and likely involving or requiring a formal premise of/to intervention

- Giving recreation models, of sacred symbols only, yet of authentic valor and ceremonial pronunciation, possibly in relation to ritualistic application towards the promotion of political order

- A clear potential need to cleanse invasive political orders not willing to allow the sacred to remain intact, unmolested, unharmed (such as political trying to prove invalidity in such a way their official policies are all degraded, over artifacts and a specialization of faith they have no approval in doctrine to incline

- Assumes political will revert to might is right, and will need to be cleansed, replaced while remaining in good industrious working order

- Political ability to disregard faith customs and still be treated properly, yet having paid, being possibly required recorded, and otherwise respecting a do not return policy (until there is a new elections)

    - Potential use of equities until a new election or state, or era is formed

- Potential conversion of sacred areas as institutional activates rented

- Potential avoidance of dead and dying at sacred site regardless of political desires, discords

- Potential relocation of dead and dying towards political areas reserved for day to day functional-practice as religious allocation

- Political empowerment as potential subjection and oppression of self, more thereby different than faith, of which is subjugated by the word as a complex dynamic, empowered through networks of facilitation, potential to experiment, as an empowerment of doing faith; yet of faith as performance driven, promises and pledges of love becoming naturally criteria of interpreting soul, an empowerment to perform as being faith

- Faith as empowered potentially with death traps, do or die allocations of/when dangerous to live either way

- Creation of delicate mazes in which to work within, highly specialized assumes the elderly enable such accords

- Political allocations of offend clerical informalities whose allocations are being hidden or chain of command therein confused for corruptive ends

- Offense as potentially limited to not breaching ownership, not invading privacy (knowing equities enables political rivals to assume moral perspective of counter torture as indicator, to a political regiment in denial of their stance as torturous

Labor maneuverability along the conformities of political short term applications as less than resilient, yet useful (thus politically, such as self-assured, as mindful approach as less than compelling to long term, cross era considerations, generally)

- Formation of wealth based specialized function groups such as for the transitioning of systems application towards national/international contractual obligations (development into vital)

- Securement of securities in proportion to economic development, instead of securities securement in guide of economic augmentation

- Preventing social reform contract to signed into religious accord/convention/doctrine-selected-tested-approved by political as so called only means, whose short term application as long term solutions is self-entitled, self-enforced, and domestic proposing international, not proving it as configuration approved as initiation (thus empiric accords sanctioned as in measure of securities distinct society)

    - Distinct society as limited to doctrine based, whose formality requires proof of beyond or not cult like performance

- Sympathetic as in connection to the formal function, and potential securement relevant to that obligation, default rights state sanctioned, in assumed promotion of working activities of organization

- Offenders against faith accepted become naturally offender to politics accepted, to what universal adaption for the conditioning towards love is there?

- Thereby without integrity as common knowledge predictably the virtue of defining love remain irrelevant, corrosive to economic development, disabler of command prompt, rather invasion attribute to command override

- Service quality as ideally speaking for itself of the determination to satisfy, to give as was paid for, and perhaps with anticipations surpassed in connectivity of future advisements in form of recommendations

- Service excellence as being rendering cliental fulfilled, such a sin joyful expectations presented as ambiance of choice

- State authority as limited to the non-interference of the enjoyment of others, such as in relation to non-criminal usage of luxury, resources

    - Potential recall of security for politicians signing into order the molestation of citizens

- Includes the use (as not sanctioned, as grounds for recordation towards political testing as systems validity verification testing) of children to benefit as sexual exploitation as if there is proof generated from unlimited resources to so called train into operational awareness disposable spies, garbage, human waste

- Assumes politicians will use stealth means to engage into tyrannical accords, such as presented to them (perhaps) as the sole means of their getting something

Highly questionable fields of labor, both in performance and attempts to solicit clients/residence as volunteer/workers

(Potential extra protections where the surveillance itself is considered a special interest group relation and coordination to/for/against workers/inmates/security and or guards, assumed applicable)

*A means to Jupiter network experimental instillations, such as to enable/disallow future entry to network core

- Hospitals as places to heal, await or recover operations

- Specialized institutions in which a person signs into required self-intervention/participation, such as to conditioning/reconditioning program

- Confining locations

- Academic tendencies attempted into experimental traditions using cult premises, especially if not registered to faith, nor the royalty

- Language interpretation centers, location created to control the quality of the language itself, such a for national or international accords

Field Marshal

(Status as security there on premise, not enabled for personal whim)

- Required to abide national tendencies

- Considered an artist derived from a traditions relating to intelligence

- Clergy required for the emergency stabilization of an area

- Used for larger festivities, those having been threatened, volunteer such as for overnight accommodations/food/after-hours usage of sampler as to encourage purchasing

- Dedicated sanitation areas, disposal sites

- Potential public prayer service if template derived from Acari (domestic technological/supreme faith, non-port, potential processing area with securities securement, facilities) archives intended as written

Heritage Principal

(Economic might across securement of regional-custom)

- Historical/Political Heritage groups as establishing what rights are founded upon, what founding father is as founding formula?

- Historical components of liberty as securement of members in ideal consideration towards the fortitude of individuality

- Models of responsible government, such as they must live for, or thus die for

- Examples of accepting brilliance, such as through liberation of tyranny and the glorification of total cleansing in the transitions of eras (predictably so)

Stellar Defense Orientated Heritage groups

(On Premise on Demand as mass mobilization potential

- Without the force of will in the amelioration of weaponry, the quota of intelligence is none (technological lead requirement, traditions declaration as bias, voids all weapons sales so that region, potentially)

- Ability along permissions to engage hostility as only means of achieving peace, in conformity that the only purpose of an invasion breach, occupy, destroy

- Access to weapons as vital as the configurations of usage, similar to the knowledgably training, self-control in relation to formalities of authoritative permissions default

- If they don't have weapons of technology, expect them to have poisons and sharp objects, what is the difference is that you think less of them and they want only more of you (what you have, without paying)

Stellar Colonial Companies as electable platforms in preparation of/to launch
- Each overall collective effort to colonize regional as one overall model

- Careful international organization as already signed for in terms of systematic faith embedded, using supreme support to guide intelligent design there forth

- If doctrine adhered to, formality of administration must core as English, language of doctrine binding cultures

- Likely assumes requirement of language control centers, likely facilitated by reformation of languages to secure English into new innovative forms of future potential leads in technological/biological, systematic faith within risen

- Assumes differing classes of function dependent on their worldly state premise as means to establish sovereignty by right of ownership/colonial development initiated upon

- Rendering opportunities affordable, incentives for participation, such as within mass ownership plans of development

- Duties (such as through usage of specific currency as an obligation) paid as required as in securement or limitations of resource in relevancy to technologies/biology and faith administrative, regional centers

- Potential mass breeding programs, such as to render an entire areas mixed in the integration of huge populations willing to become a new race, onto species allocation, if required such as for sovereignty accords of biological independence, or as terms of treaties

- Potential leeway as enabling mass small business ventures, such as for the solidification of nationhood, such as under premise of faith as theme, chosen, tried, and truth

- Market base for projection of colonization, enabled such as with this state doctrine in inclusion to systematic faith overall

- Potential midway arrivals of networking Jupiter Principal Binding (as empirical securement stations/centers) into anticipated colonial thereafter branching across vast areas compelling to develop

- Empathies on securing communications (empirical as multinational in origins), such as requiring media and other subscriptions as or tariffs in securement of defensive technological application

- Securement of agricultural and other specific specialized resource/production orientated planets/sectors

- Reserves in securement of Supremes' mobilization, deliverance of staple goods, and a prediction-action-control database for attempts at marketplace to impose monopoly tactics, as a tyrannical means to control as sneak attack at vital points of development

- Potential limitations or requirement of specific market standards defaults, such as the thereby productions model center of production supreme

- Elite reserves as possibly limited to Jupiter, such as in scheduled patronage accord for the development and upgrade inclusion as a network of most advance science available, assumed

- Assumes some leeway between markets and civics in regards to vitals, and or cost adjustments therein

- Potential capping of how much agricultural products may be distributed towards cliental, yet allowing ongoing continual purchasing assumed

        - Limits on reselling, or limits on cross border bypass as peaceful

- Limitations on the sudden and system wide degrading of all stock quality as peaceful, especially if based on so called sudden inclusion of special interest persons (indicator of invasion)

- Notification of so called midnight reshuffling of administrative persons, or overnight policy input by covert means, such as thereby bypassing democratic or contractual limitations

    - Emergency public/authoritative notification inquiry

- General liberty-trade as factoring in formal formulas embedded in an overall configuration as systematic order, whose development is encouraged by development plans whose patriotism includes economic endeavor potential

Stellar Colonial Science - Investigative Scouts

- Projection of distribution resources required per allocations and usage of an energy system

- Establishing exchange rates rendering vitals feasible, onto scheduled potential or inventories depletion predictors

- Liberal trade as secured by empiric instillations requiring a minimal of scheduled trade, and anticipated potential of hostilities

- How much coverage would be required to maintain an ongoing, unlimited supply line, such core to each system/sector, and smaller redistribution across secondary core routes assumed also of vital strategic importance?

- Potential to map stability of routes, or know which areas become dangerous, including containment blockades

- Cognitive/automated. Synthetic-override enhancements for hosting abilities dedicated to securities-enacted or secured as leisure, both for areas where no service is acceptable

- Technological samples as exemplifying nations/worlds, and potentially their empires of faith, such as in conformity to the themes of selected

- Trade designed for the mutual expansion, development of regions as requiring vital interlinks along reverses, such as to indicate huge vulnerabilities for strategic counter invasive standards of appreciation (enjoyment of binary system configurations)

- Assumes differences in power usage and overall resources can create completely distinctive systems for operations/supportive-culture, meanwhile remain cohabited as in God's direction.

- Assumes production offset (conflicting materials merged with new methods of overall technology therein innovative and unheard of, breakthrough as previously unknown), due to being different might enable secondary production lines in which both formations are supportive requirements to the emerging technological, or traditions trend

- Specialized institutions interpreting economic opportunity for commercial advancement, enabling references instead of loose net council members nevertheless expected in liaison function to their domestic leadership

- Color-code mapping practicality of strategic development, for ease of prioritizing explanation, such as of pricing for goods and services rendered

    - Attention to quick shifts of practical as era forging relevance or of invasive standards otherwise not known, not intended obvious

- Danger test runs, creating canary ships, including generating false sensors, false reading, and false data of all kinds yet of no level of authoritative value or identification

- Potential options to bring in patriotic adjustments, enhancements, and potential security reinforcement to neutralize corrupting political agency attempting to downgrade overall faith science by virtue of economical configuration

- In-region, on-world fabrication of market securement devices

- Mapping system compatibility in regards to manufacturing standards, assumes adaptive leeway enables considerable systematic component unification into systems accordance as virtue in wholesome results rendered, upgrade potential assumed total/limited as in compliance compute-accord

- Monitoring of biologically based hiring schemes, such as to identify if some races/species are only willing to hire their own, yet some with the banner of all/most/diverse accepting, diversified

    - A secondary examination on the availability due to assumed highly specialized work/labor

- The potential to enable nations/worlds to subsidize workers as quick incentive for transitional progress into conforming technological/biological integration programs

- Assumes non relevant world may not subsidize workers to be automatically special interest at the living/mindful expense of low level ability to function

- Assumes that if there is nearly none having the specialized expertise, their economy already favors a transitional move to be worthwhile, and the subsidized values are thereby predictably agents and spies there to extract

- Calculating costs per configurations, as well as configurations per transports, such as to exemplify whether specific models should be made in larger volumes and cosmetically enhanced to differentiate custom-application/function

- Assumes ships have form arrangement, colors, lighting to distinguish their labor/specialist relevant function

- An examination of regions/worlds where differing attempts of administration have not resulted in establishing economic stability/production standards expected for the available resources, efforts, skill or potential of labor

- An examination of core configurations vs/ policy interpretation, such as auditing political motto for potential corruptive negligence

     - A mapping of problems found vs. taxes

- Assumes taxation problems are relevant to attempts to defund securities and securement configurations, therein what is are core of those configuration

- Testing for potential hostile threats attempting to rise covertly, such as among massing into lower ranked/standards of authoritative might/negligence

- Strategize awareness as in virtue of connectivity to withstanding systems control, assumes Yahweh systems (Integrity Matrix) may oversee/override with alert prompt stellar transit permissions, such as to lock down a sector, route, transfer segments to safe approach/horizons if applicable/configured for catastrophe, yet in securement with formalities and premise

- Mapping, promoting packaged inventive towards discovery/educational opportunities

- Field research potential across various functions (augmentation of resource wealth, of referencing wealth, proof in testament of will/career, pledge based fulfillment such as establishing trade/traditions value

- Defining clearly responsibilities and potential rewards, including means to generate on site entrepreneur bids

- Assumes storage is limited, resources limited, empowerment of workers thereof limited

Great-Opportunities Network - Stellar

- Electable such as into crypto currency invest minimum sum capable, maximum until expansions notice into specialized projects accorded, initiate, launch!

- Research into development options, crypto invest, experiment, maintain permanent (assumed sellable) royalties ownership

- Opportunities for educators in reliance with, possibly required as accord within long term industrial projects planning (guarantee of specialized, qualified labor)

- Tactical conquest allocations, such as securities and patrol, defend capture, own.

- Baiting fortresses as boarded no matter what, nation/world of origins requiring a safety, self-destruct core such as at own peril of fabrication (required functional, or in damaged retreat if ejected for defensive counter measure, should include other systems depending on ramming potential/regional precedence

- Potential faith and performance, high priority performance, including dangerous areas or further as registered to securities baiting program

    - Assumes jealously is not a rime

- Assumes public services not impeded, or otherwise carefully contracted, such as using mercenary contract privilege/obligation

- Mass reformation projects, such as agricultural, touristic, national emergency reserves

Communications Facility

- Maintaining signal with no usable data besides operational continuity of utilities as functioning, secured, scheduled service/being-serviced

- Subjection of update patches, equipment, as implement, hack, signal verification

- Assumes the system can turn momentarily on and off at differing intervals and measure if there are signals beyond default specified standards for operation, along hardware/software conformities of usage, with scheduled performance relevant maintenance, including refreshment

- Embedded in accordance to default commercial value, traffic, and thereby rendered of a mobile, transferable form/ease-of usage

- Trade as dependent partially on trade supply volumes of domestic (national/worldly), along international resources, thereby establishing industry wide open communications of reserved vital, such as contractual (assumes technological leading nations/worlds have specific needs required addressed and thereby limit biological to model samples of relevancy as standard to lesser populations maintaining resource driven endeavors required long-term stabilized such as into stellar accord, and traditions nations/worlds require as example templates made rather than so called mass abundance of technology

- Limiting food for materials to natural disaster sites, such as to include disaster wreckage (avoids reuse as fake disaster-scenario building)

- Verification of all formalities of communication across supreme power structures, to map and tract overall pledges, mottos, headlines and reports formal indicating

    - Mass breeding programs and volumes

- Desired to render inner regions independent, to what associable custom-regional means of altered regulations formal (calculating economic long term consequence)

- Finding worries, concerns over status of commercial favorability in prediction/projection to specific development standards/statements

- Mapping tariffs, especially if they are creating boundaries seemingly only unfair (not serving a purpose to secure such a sin correlation of high salaries therein required adjusted)

- Assumes forcing class distinction is a means of molestation/so-called-extraction through desperation

- Auditing whether there are claims the people are being taken care of, potential conquest protocol allocations (wrath accords)

- Political obsession of interpersonal habits as endlessly breaching privacy as invasive yet to no formalities acceptable (anti own convention, mottos, stated concerns as signs of tyranny/treason)

- Reminder that the capital areas have little to no expectation on/for privacy, and rather in scheduling and arranging options within sanctuary settings configurable/reserved

- Generalization, if they are allowed by law, or of the government create agents to enact a behavior, such behavior is intended patriotic as default accord (relevant to the dignity of the nation, assumed)

- Industrial/policy complaint submission of unfair, unusable policies, licensing standards, applicability do to unwarranted or irrelevant usage of territory such as due to weather, regional obligations, and every day sightings of specific occurrence

- Potential need to access, enable highly specialized contractor style databases of information in regards to industry standards on processing, solutions coordination, and adaptive features and options development

Cultivating Intelligence
Domestic automated micromanagement potential

(Potentially emergencies capitalist, small business easement, securement accord/program)

- Advantage through neighbors participation in production potential (small business plan builder, easement to enable licensing, registration of smaller ventures)

- Touristic easement of regional resource/options known as craft/custom selections (specifically small groups, services (non-corporate, non-organized as remote, cyclical, such as seasonal)

  - Performance talent within specific limited traveling distances

- For areas where remote locations at mercy of few educated peoples, other high paying trades, and otherwise being considered a quick or doomed extraction site by those working and not investing as licensed, as cultural standard, of generally abusive occupation of lands such as having historic grievances regionally

- Relieving so called temporary monopolies which are limiting the expansion and development of remote communities

- Assumes remote area is overpriced yet local resources of impoverished is not developed, yet the so called rich are heavily subsidized (assumes resource extraction enabled infrastructure development and now subsidization into touristic areas is being blocked, such as to avoid fines from breach of licensing terms, and other *needless large scale damages to ecology, biology

- Predicts the use of technology to overcome infrastructural limitations is not being subsidized regionally as having invested interest for a few individual to monopolize

- See if bloodlines of monopoly match, and thereby an informal royal system is being imposed to oppress the local population

- Predicts a general resentment on being practical to new comers to the area, such as of conspiracies to ruin an entire location and gain ownership cheaply, by also buying cheap corruptive criminal forces to chase away, harm, harass local population

- Enabling local asset development to cheapen components/process development mechanism/device to render production effective (effective resource processing as regional upgrade)

Regional labor Resource
Employment seeker registry/listings

- Listed strength (grouped into common function/premise)

- Craft skills and attached samples, experience

- Formal accreditation/formal-training

- Regional asset listings, such as: Easement/storage easement in relation to tools and material if applicable/possible

    - Consideration of storage costs, durability of storage economically, ability to be secure

- Management persons available/availability, such as part time with potential transitioning to long-term

- Problem solving specialists/semi-specialists among the selection

- General labor potential as searchable group

- Labor potential/skill by machine experience

- Labor potential/skill based on specific equipment

- Labor potential/skill by locations/settings worked in

- General labor specific language assessment

Securement against Corruption
(Predictable invasion tactics/ stealth adherence into formal results bound)

- Supreme influences of faith as standardized in alignment to faith as long term projection signed into, locked in as (demands, desires-emotional outbursts to dismantle as urgent guarded against, whose content is from invasion, in regards to ongoing mass organization such as by differing names linked with a commonality among separated language/symbols/serial markings, assumed)

    - Assumes if faith is not being attacked or not critical against invasion, they are already occupied

- Sanctuary properties as registered and on premise, therein breaches upon a secured and monitored area, predictably signifies invasion uses heavily camouflaged means of also disrupting validity of securities embedded

- Requiring formalities of intervention, informalities as highly questionable, until the system itself, if, is found tampered with/into (wrath protocols)

    - Predictably, systematic faith as design is used to create counter designs, to promote objectives as dystopian, to render emotional a reason argument, to give others priority where the signed into faith is by virtue a source of principal approved as intended bound/binding-principal into

- To what level of convenience is there as overall advantage to adhering patriotic, or have invasive tactics downgraded domestic identity as hostile, yet the invasion as mass movement somehow protected, even encouraged?

    - Assumes media depictions where the sentiments and ideas of others are in promotion of bypassing domestic as natural, expected, even desired, such as in affirmation of thus no longer, or rendered unprotected sign/symbols of political, faith symbols, meanings, historic significance once taken for granted as a strong cultural stabilizer, granted a shift of eras is a reason for leeway

- Potential remedy, use of societal passion to enable test site festivities enabling the celebration of domestic values as major filter for/of appreciation

- Assumes local foods, sites sounds enjoyed, patriotism expected enjoyable from both notably domestic and visitors alike

- Assumes abridging of faith embedded civics peace desired within initiation of event/parade/celebration

- Liberty as meaning secured areas, where freedom of consumption meets securement of ride home, such as within fees of entry to provide individual, group, or select case by case departures

- Community speaking as in continuity of being public service, regarding invoking societal passion

- Economical as respecting area in recommendation of feedback, respect to hosts, enjoyment of civic duty, with leeway on pledging remedies or future contributions of remedy as return to the investment of charitable care giving (things will happen, explanations are to be had)

- Potential for privet enterprise to form overall lines/territory of event occupation, such as for member only approaches, or select invite, or requires orientation known and possibly tested

- Potential profit making booths/goods-services, yet recommended warning of pricing, or easement of paid in advance, to using event currencies, such as potential easement of licensing/record-keeping

- Potential civics remedy, coins creation allowance, such as upon 5th year anniversary

       - Assumed to promote nationalism

- Talk of administration of nation as regarding what has been created as good for the while nation, if possible

- Practical as likely citing 8 hour max duration, yet potentially transitioning into another kind of festivities for scouts program to attend, entering, such as to require them to clean up

- If heavy profit, donation, left over supplies, giving distribution of/minimum-wage or wage-minimum as bonus to volunteers. If economic and not patriotic, than perhaps it can be about making money? Reminder author never once received substantially from state at point of writing this doctrine, possible a handful of books total.

- Reminder of wage amounts, not indicative of work or efforts involved, as recommended attached to show internationals, with thank you! (If large bonus, we appreciate you!)

- *Drunks as expected not to comprehend long-term implications (based on movability, ability to communicate, ability to reach sanitation)

- Taking the complaints of drunks seriously and with leeway, safety security, ideally as family (rescued as leaving, yet who?)

- Potentially focusing on municipal nations a on premise and or national (national recommended for inviting many international visitors, such as to showcase industrious functional culture)

- Recommended vitals not sold if relevant to function celebration, yet luxury versions allowed, and being careful such as ordering in advance of participation to avoid conflict over stock volumes

- Example, natives receiving or giving/providing (also such as state sanctioned, or to promote local staple food, such as for thanks-giving

  - Assumes inter-communities share-bonding events potential

  - Raffles, prizes, contests, such as voting over produce, arts, production samples

- Civics support as tables, booths, monitoring of equipment such as to activate/record upon damages

- Creating sites specifically for students, separating high school, collage, university from professionals/performers

  - Creating time zoning, such as to increase sound depths, ability to sell intoxication

- General censorship of pro injustice, satire as shut your mouth

Economy Core
(Wage Determination in reflection to contextual application)

- Purpose and function in relation to training and specialized expertise, ongoing interest required to maintain updated/relevant

- Contextual Clarity: What subsidy/welfare programs is the state offering completion exclusive rights/access/privilege, such as regarding multinational implications of foreign nationals supported, and domestic fighting over titles

- Are those working an attraction, does the overall endeavor as company culture translate to effecting the system positively/negatively

- Can brand quality be maintained with the "level" of workers, level as in relevance to required bureaucratic control?

  - Assumes technology based workers are better trained through habitual equipment from complex lifestyle formations, and that traditions potentially segment in easement of work due to number of workforce, as differing styles of comprehension required and contextual lifestyle thereof involved

    - Example food intake

    - Example relationship standards

- Example need to be more to less sensitive between coworkers, assumed mass population of non-specialist nature relates to historically disposable virtues, cultures of appearance rather than results (managed, collective corrections as traditions strength, yet potentially sever weakness as assumed standard anyone/everyone can be replaced regarding those of highly specialized function/nature)

- Knowledge of consequence as given within lifestyles addressing layers and cycles of training/education, cultivation

- Are those making wages disqualifying the overall validity of the labor as end of day celebration, such as to seemingly validate pillaging?

- Does comfort provide rest such as to reenergize, prolong endurance or is work stalled

- Are those testing the differences themselves monitored for tampering?

Industry Enhanced training of security/enforcement as knowledge per industry of conduct/operation/methodology

- Industry specific protection groups as managed by those having enhancing observational, intervention or relevant work skill, such as to contribute helpful commentary along report building, of an overall effective, highly specialized avenue/nature of operational harmony/rendering

- Sever shortage as requiring adjustment of policy, contracts, such as to determine validity of management/paperwork/supply lines and other potential third-party involvement

- Establishing reactionary advice rendering, warnings/alert of status, such as in membership connectivity to systems of operations, example of Jupiter Principal Binding as research development and mass resource distribution, assumed

- Requiring the ability to check, determine validity of formal premise, such as in measuring the responsibilities undertaken by those having administrative control

- Safeguards across democratically short term development in relation to industries, and potential misdirection in which an essential or vital factor is translated into misdirection, such as seemingly towards abandonment

- Safeguards against tyrannies domestic and international, using democratic slogans to force a collective blessing as validation to enforce (unjust) might (beware of those using vague convention as validation for brute policy bypass)

- Warning on the implications of joining predictably corrosive industrious formations, such as those without a safety such as in literal terms policies to manage hazards, enable safety features and other technology based requirements of quality environmental control (ventilation, first aid, hazards referencing, and emergency action/response stations)

- Potential organization of producers to create processing, production centers, such as to arrange land features to form a supply chain formation and or onto station to station production line style of enterprise/venture

- Potential crypto stocks as seasonal and capped both in amounts sold, amounts earned and amounts losable (assumed based on infrastructure/asset securities as well as reserve stocks secondary (perhaps requiring safety features and securities/device monitoring)

- Capitalist as a having long term consequence worthwhile for the regional-custom application of developmental projects, thereby the region will, would increase in capital worth beyond/despite productions as assumed requirement of reasonability, and potentially required regional transformative projects, or incites need for land reformation or land salvation projects

- Industry wide simplified and linked with formalities of policy presented, relevant to operational standards of conformity adjustment

Economy Core Labor
Conditions Feedback

- Feedback as exemplifying validity of specific policies, procedures sent forth/received from government/supreme/specialized or formal interested organization and or leaderships applicable (potential members input and formality, required)

- Feedback on comfort levels in relations to standard policies proposed, such as does not match cultural, geographical, or regional-custom, plus referencing, mapping

- Degrading of workshop environments, of emergency aid or relief efforts (assumes organized, invasive, use of technological and or traditions strategies to dissatisfy public survey/feedback/performance-rendering)

- Issues in economic efficiencies

- Requests for emergency support towards the mass organization/venturing of workers "piling up", of regional disorganization in which large numbers of domestic labor forces are being ignored, such as by monopoly trends of local larger families/companies trying to artificially reduce the local community, such as by rendering vitals and infrastructure dysfunctional to impede (tampering/molestation of waterworks, sanitation, energy, communications, schemes to reduce touristic appeal such as under guise of hate or anti-hate)

- Issues with statistical information, does not match physical or demonstrable realities of the region, such as to submit media to examine claims of validity

- Demands of producers to increase freedoms of a location by restoring wild/wilderness state of the area, such as within context of territorial markers, arrangements as liberty in securement of integrity

Economy Core Requests to Glorify

- Requests to create economic relevant museum

- Conversion of commercial, residential, industrial, stellar spacing towards regional trade good models/displays, such as instead of creating too costly of an overall conversion/restoration of area beyond aesthetic and securement of foundations/pillar support

- Marveling site as introduction, displaying highly appraised, emerging greatness and wonderment

Economic-Cultural Themes to Glorify

- Salvation through economic order/intervention

- Teaching fundamentals of value assignment to core cultural meanings, in relation to political abridgements to civics and or faith orderly

- Concept of eternity in regards to economic applicability of transformative capital building

- Examples of economically qualified ameliorations of regions against tyrannical, invasive forces, without explaining the false titles (assumed due to the complexity and secrecy of the inner configurations, thereby sealing itself into secret and supporting/supported by contradiction) or facets beyond failed royalty trends under guide of mass special interest, or mass securities perpetuated for the sole aim/augmentation as order clause and premise (enforced by hypocrisy, deceit, non-formality, and general distortion and degrading of faith, civics, politics, as main indicator proven further therein economically)

    - Assumes corruption within/as the securities and public-welfare or government aid, as example, fabricate the very dystopian conditions they themselves war against, defeating therein all locals while suffering mildly on both conflicting sides, yet possibly at their peril due to emergency civics policies creating stealth engagement protocols therein)

- The economic stabilities, enhancements, refinements brought about author as systematic Christ, compelling integrity abridgment and systematic order, in appreciation to God's direction, defining God's being as alive and collector of souls

- An appreciation to those generous in terms of honoring liberty as model securement standards included/involved

- Encouraging the sanctity of marriage, such as into economic (material) display of abridging regional bloodlines into transitions of standards binding/tribute of/to faith/civics manifestation or automated relevance of validity as verified, accords compute, conform compliance reached

- Examining purpose and interpretations along eras of transformative action/consequence, in relation to economical formation/operations/results of production/lifestyles/specialized functions (exemplifying market progress)

- Salvation clause in display, as having wealth (compromise/pledge/contractual) to devote into/as (depletion of reserves specified) restorative usage of resources such as to fulfill specific therein obligations to redeem a physical location/systems-application, potentially as standing order in consignment of truth rendered manifest

- Displays of the universe as a whole, exhibiting the slender of resources, natural stellar formation, potential venture sites if applicable (attachments to Jupiter perhaps required)

- Themes of being in God's direction through affirming clear thought in context of the overall abridging connection intended/in-designs of systematic faith/order

- Potential examples of less than clear thought, yet whose configuration and rather results are clearly on premise, and the sense of liberty provided in validation of questionable yet validated integrity (assumes maturity content such as of using controlled substances/devices/medications and other augmentations

- Does not necessarily justify non-compatible bios forging direct of DNS/circuitry bypass/partial faith quoting, rather promotes enhancing experimental recognition/awareness stimulation-input (as intended self-infliction not extending as corrosive to others)

- Critical cultural-historic points of transformative acceptance into technological/biological/systematic order, as phases of strategic awareness

Cannabis and Sedatives
(Recreational Allocations)

- The assumption that ancient faith is probably right/correct as affirming the default pot herbs usage of cannabis and sedatives, such as when economically feasible

- Limited in accordance to securements to protect workforce, such as in maintaining high production quality standards

- Enabling special monitoring/intervention capability based on organized tendencies to invade, disrupt, takeover covertly

- Assumes larger industrious productions require standard acceptance/appreciation/policies-to-secure creational usage as well as product development in relation to energy, medicines, fabrics, other material forms

- Control of image as control of overall product usage, such as to instill model behavior as formalities, and by adding non-standard drugs, criminal deception, and alcohol, demonstrating contextual awareness of misuses, likely/recommended among satirical usage

- Limiting usage as regular diet in connection to standard and every day usage of other staple/mass-available products such as assumed also allowed coffee, tea, sugar

- Potential refinement of product or standard device implemented for usage as perhaps recommended

- Potential civics ordinance depicting where such as outside usage in context of not using a device

- Disallowance of faith to comment that cannabis itself ruins the soul, yet conduct in appreciation to custom regional, and economic values assumed not in question

- Usage to promote love and joy as manifestation of God's natural bounty, such as in reflective pose, and general poetic pose

- If smell of cannabis prohibited, other smells especially spice-food, allergy, disease, and bio/chemical/chemical also to be prohibited

- Assumes over consumption/presence of various usage all disruptive, and incense the main justification of non-usage yet of perfume similar to being a pot herbs substance

- Assumes creating hungry atmospheres without satisfying alone is generally counter productive

- Assumes there are areas on site dedicated to the allowance of activity causing scents, possibly as required for standards to be policy

    - Potential exact listing of deodorants, food scents, incense flavors allowed on location

    - Potential authoritative allowances, as formal criteria contractual rendered

    - Potential overuse/saturations-measurement standards to exclude ability to impose scent and claim inability to control, conform, comply

- Activities in contemplation/direction to what, establishing premise, *receiving what you paid for

- Faith usage as themed, potentially regulated in differing contextual application of securement, therein once approved for usage the soul regards fulfillment of pledges/oaths/conceptual frameworks and design

- Potential adult-baptismal themes

Industrial Process as:
- Extraction

- Refinement

- Adapting labor to equip-suit/predict resource potential and availability such as in reflection of market values to sell/trade as commodity

- Transformative designs - Research and development

    - Resource substitution experimentation

    - Resource supply chain, processing efficiency considerations

    - Adapting to differing regional environment, establishing model types

- Relevant function based using similar or same components (what can be made with what we have, as we expand the inventory of what we use/can-use

    - Luxury models potential

    - Inter-compatibility clause, as enabling greater systems of device, modes, accessories

- Potential security measures, adaptation required as per increase of overall value/economic-worth

- Liberty seeking and conservative as reserves secured administrative tendencies, including domestic to international standards of consideration (establishing operational configurations)

    - Investment panels, voting panels

    - Emergency procedures, quality control standards

    - Licensing and regulatory conditions

Science Core

- Estimating the value of investigation, inquiry

- Exploring which field of observation is possible, and potentially creating conduct related policies/agreement per strategic usage of specialist

- Establishing/refining compartments of responsibility, such as in adaptive ease of scheduling, coordinating, securing among individuals, rendering works more efficient

- Family life, practicality considerations, such as potential on-site/near-site living accommodations

- Appointing guardians to enforce during vulnerable times such as in celebration, regarding payment or visitation of inventories

- A warning on tests/research regarding poverty areas, of probable long standing criminal organization, required political, faith, civics adjustments secure, including a securities and other authority cleanse (do not go, assumed)

- An internal filter, science core being concerned with science? Or of the ravings of lunatics

Civics Core Qualifier

- How much ownership, power do the local brewers, drug manufacturers, and other intoxication and possibly criminal enterprises in the area?

    - Formal policies, regulation, abridging securities clearances (assumed formal and or traceable)

- Is the banking system secure?

- What environmental practices/assessment standards are there in place for industrial production?

- Whom are considered important founders of the region, what is their story?

- What is the closest doctrines of usage in the region, how does the area react/treat those people, and to what meaning/values does their configuration attribute the importance of wealth in compliance or compatibility to faith prescribed/preached-formally

    - Do media depictions of the area match the quality of performance in that region?

- Whom creates the largest transfers of resources for charity, does it affect their competition?

- What are the main routes of production outward, do the major nearest intersect appear to involve invasive standards of participation?

- What kind of civics expositions do they have?

- What kind of academic investments or rewards are issued to the domestic students there? (What specialized avenue of interest and or what does it appear in relation to biology/technology/systematic order

- How are the local natives treated?

- Cost of goods having to transfer boundaries, or otherwise cross into territorial securities/transit securement sites

- Is there any national, civics, faith or other forms of organized enthusiasm?

    - What rights are associated?

- What kind of energy options are there?

- What is their version of equality vs. liberty and the application of faith?

- What are their formal studies/reports on their domestic economic issues?

Capital Policies

- Is the area regulated against conspiring nationals/multi-national formations?

- Is there talk about fighting for an end to exploitation? *Capital assumed too expensive for non-exploiters/wealth to participate

- Assumes use of advanced configurations and stature gained from market place basis for being named as so called exploiter

    - Assumes envy is the feeling of being exploited

- Assumes accusers have created no remedies, overall critics recommended if not required to contain solutions rendering, or content applicable for securities emergency simulation, in considerations obvious

- Are there people following member's coming to report security concerns such as national, international operations/coordination of?

- Are children conducting agent like operations, children assumed able to perform scout like hostilities, as in having spy formations of training

- Are domestic authorities unable to control themselves from threatening an emerging person of influence, perpetuating similar to a societies of influence

- Are the rules practical?

- Is there extra securities, regulations where the rules/indication/unusual infrastructure are not practical?

- Are there luxury pawnshops to move goods not usually sellable or kept based on pricing? Assumed securable

- Formal benefits as in-house, not mentioned to public, kept from broadcast, yet possibly registered with securities (assumes premium cost across capital)

- Requirement to have preapproved configurations of proposed trade (limits, assignable values for negotiation/transaction) of loans, bonds, industrial credit, mortgage-ratings, reserves-validity-certificate, within entry

- On person data expected secured as high priority asset for carrying reserves summaries, currency stipulation, clear industry (owners, representatives) guidelines

- No asking, requesting during recreations/celebrations, visit as special interest, celebrity citing, such as during entire visitation

  - Transit as required driven, monitored

  - Verification on supply/reserve-holdings claims, so many destinations, to what productions are they reserved, contracted for?

  - Verification of supplier/reserve-holdings debts in relation to stated worth

- What are the proposed terms for a network/systems status as liberty trade (securement of technological, traditions & inter designed mechanisms)

  - Tariff issues/benefits?

Economic-Cultural Protection Pacts
Liberty Core

- To what terms of protection occupies the forces of tranquility/securities/cultural reinforcement (supreme societies of influence)

- What domestic principals for/for reserves are there, establishing safeguards for the markets and its clients, predictably involves vitals for living, and career/reinforcing cultural infrastructure as traditions/technological

- In what manner is liberty trade present, whereas free-trade seems the equivalent of being merchant in the wilderness which may have its own recruiting/evolving strategic values?

- What allowances are there between domestic goods/services and international/multinational goods/services, especially in relation to vitals and

- Free trade as assumed exploitive without regards to securities, currency, border, or domestic protection accords

- What protection/heritage groups and their principles and premise, are there in the securement of the economy in virtue of civilization as directed among empires of faith

- Do the meanings of cultural doctrines include calibration of values, reflective of a harmonious configurations of faith, civics to political accords (orderly?)

- How much cultural emphasis is there on victimizing own system or its elite?

- What formal reasoning is there for the imposition of tariffs, and therein are there remedies and limitations automated in connection to situational awareness/infrastructure development from an economic/industrial-expansion front

- Transitions of liberty into security as converting wilderness at dangers of savage, to the securement in safety and abundance so called tame/raw-resource-readiness as pastoral

- What arrangements are there for the overall expansion of?

- What safeguards and liberty in form of options defended by regulation/policy enforced are there relating to relationship and procreation

- What industry by industry or sector by sector custom policy/arrangements are there for production?

- What tracking, monitoring, method of mythology are there within transportation/commerce and it's inventories, means of communication, and port or mid transit transferring protocols?

    - Potential limitation of ports as domestic only, for retrieval and redistribution

- International monitoring/live-oversight assumed in compliance to infrastructural investments grating access/privilege to secure economic trade

- Red flag/caution-alert for policy based on political motto which is considered void, degraded, or empty title/empty significance simply repeated over and over as so called convincing

- Automated symbols and inventoried as national mottos written on any products, such as domestic and international as systems embedded (internationally recommended) accord

    - Potential delay during transit to safe keep item whereabouts

Duties as Tariffs

- Imposed to finance facilitation requirement in appeasement to the quality of life standards of regionally grouped workers, whose otherwise breaching upon client nations as repulsed and oppressed becomes subject to interpretation as invasive and disregarding national contractual obligations

- Potential defaults allocated to education, such as for the promotion of specialists

- Potential requirement as war time protocol, yet whose duration is assumed easily sinister, as not meant the sole means of economically supporting the conflict or so called conquest, thereby suspect of pillaging

- Creating protected display, easy access references for market relevant user/owners/interpreters

- Duties and tariffs as a mottos relevant issue rather than a direct motto as limitation of political mastery of convention and linguistic implications so fourth

- Ecological securement, yet recommended capitalist in formation such as to secure waters and implement fishing population, to secure air and be safeguarding agriculture, medicine, and intelligence/biological formation (such as within fetal development)

- Predictable sectors for tariffs

- Raw resource extraction trade amounts vs. reserved entry specific per industry-wide usage, assumed applicable

- Trades formation and development, such as requiring international contract/obligations-configurations to allow

- Energy formation and development, such as requiring international contract/obligations-configurations to allow

- Highly specialized as rare academic, intelligence or other intellectually derived configuration-standard, such as vital/pivotal/fulfilling for civilization

- Fabrics creation, such as safeguarding larger manual labor forces by requiring domestic upgrading along trade removing tariffs, or imposing tariffs for that endeavor specifically yet sharing technologies such as to increase and forge multinational standards of trades into traditions forming/expansion

- Tariffs to requires accountability as requested feature for cross border disputes, (potentially a minimalist sums attached), as a means of additional or only records keeping, with compliance requirement

Infrastructural Evaluations Core

- An examination of supply lines relevant to commercial mass transit

- Mapping rates vs. status/capability of transit lines

- Mapping adaptation features abridging transit lines, such as from port to road/rail/passageway

- Rating overall transit speeds vs. specified and otherwise ability to

- Assumes moderate as medium to high-medium usage/acceleration set as optimum longstanding performance drive

- Low or green, as casual and possibly heavy, heavy load equaling to medium therein medium equal to high-medium, assumed

- Emergency provision/policies, distribution models

- Rate of road depletion, associated rates or trade relation scheduling routes as mapped

- Automated road conditions survey, such as at designated locations, or looking for specific patterns of degradation/usage

- Connection to relevant economic cores, such as scientific as default verifier

- Regional industrial strengths in regards to owner resources and references, assumes of a secured referencing, membership requirements assumed

    - How to lobby correctly the political, recommendations, standards, regulations/implications

    - No informal investigations such as on preferred clients, nor informal custom arrangements

        - Assumes contractual as terms for due diligence, as also do diligently

- Potential contractual note disbanding efforts to "water-down", remove filters to augment volume at expense of stable brand quality

- Requiring industry wide standards to enable worker investment opportunities along general salaries raising beyond desperate or vulnerable among excessive as overlapping systems of wealth, including international

- Signifying if a company invests only in security as to control the working environment yet not securement of comports, security, while holding lock-down contracts, these are indicators of securities whose mandate is solely for self-expansion as only concern (typically royal like), therein using figurehead/political-figures as centralized standard whose predeveloped responses to hide as inner-conspiracy. Thereby does free speech rephrase out of context, out of era potential reconsideration of long term projection versus simplicities of obey, perform duty, and be diligent.

- Applies to unions using privileges to seize control through attempted or appointed control sessions

- Overlapping as meaning, if workers must occupy an increasing number of responsibilities which enable wealth to augmented dramatically, salary and or benefits adjustments not met, may require political intervention to release contractual patronage obligations

- As meaning, great wealth generation will cause international criminal and invasive conspiracy to target company and workers, and not securing the workers, such as to take their intellectual contributions is akin to abiding invasion (potentially)

> - Indicators, loss of registry

> - Rapid lost and death of workers or owners

- Unexplained succession of unqualified workers into ownership along or followed by heavy loss or reduction to brand image/quality/stability features

- Owner and workers as enabled through faith intelligence, implementation of standardization of do not entry, breach entry into death traps, as salary/benefits adjustments recommended if no offer from the options above can be reached, are deemed to qualify

> - Perpetual stalemates appreciated welcome

- Potential administrative/work-area/research development/storage inventory/luxury transportation (static options recommended required) usage of do no breach area

- Requiring monitoring and safety protocols, such as only available during scheduled off/maintenance hours

- Invasion or corruption economically felt as a lowering of efficiency, monitoring the abrupt rising cost of good/services alongside increased amounts of defective quality production, inability to fulfill contractual obligations, such as to forwards to non-relevant third parties, inability to advance processing methods (such as ingenious owners/development teams have been cleansed)

- Companies being merged into monopoly formations, after, during an emergency or epidemic circumstance, as default test bodies for poisoning and or lack of bodies

- Examining for ID suppression, inability/lack of desire from political to intervene as included as a tyranny rising (securities centralized as engaging day and night yet hidden, with special interest occupying administratively day and night, such as tying up and (predictably) becoming a blockade against foreign both corrupt as for degradation, and in title to prevent degradation of domestic brands across industries of previous realization)

- Examining political maneuvering in attempts to legitimize industry wide monopolies, such as try and merge production supreme as one company, instead of one service application abiding many owners/formations

- Bribery as predictably point of entry into total replacement

Production Supreme

Expected concentration of reference inventories

- Development of work safety per industry, per custom regional applications as problem solving directory/inventory

- Easement of coordination to bridge across territorial borders, such as to access simplified direction, policies of concern and have complex contractual obligations filtered by an intelligence program, if applicable/ready for such standard of service

- Aid with those using so called authoritative allowances to harm their companies, easement to verify credentials/premise verification of authoritative/securities figure

- Examining the soundness of public announcement, such as from so called political accords, such as of so called high stature (assumes claims of do and don't tell or else)

- Verifying the quality determination standard of completeness in terms of previously signed for/acclaimed public policy, such as in regards to environmental clean-up, pledges to support local communities or respect regional custom, such as under contractual obligations

- Promoting inter-industry formality mechanisms such as forwarded into the supreme requests and proposals *for template designs applicable to all industrial once configured into compliance with systematic order

- Creating collective price empowerment, such as to match, confront international standards of binding partnership proposed as fair/equitable

- Specialist vs. manual labor argument ground of examination of invasive counter measures as thus formal warfare applied

- Denouncement of aggressive suppression at completions, such as in formation of political awareness that the nation is being divided, and God is likely already being degraded using associated investments to downgrade media, education, and instill turmoil/fake emotional movements bypassing reason/convention/civic obligation

- Heritage groups as defining long term in connectivity to God's image a requiring clear definitions of/for integrity and love, along compatible obligations/policy summaries, a such as in binding principal/feature of specialized networks of integrated designs

- Instilling the meaning of trade and a richness in options, performance standards, availability and selectable choice as a proportional direction of so called short term constant updating, whose long term faith requirement involves doctrines of a complex nature, such as this one. Introducing liberty grounds ti exemplify liberty-trade

- Population volumes are needed known, to adjust, plan for economic propulsion

- A careful consideration that rising strengths/system-designs among individuals otherwise posed to rise/boom-increase within mass populated areas of similar resources yet heavily distributed into long established systems, will want to refugee into leader technological nations only to be naturally oppressed by so called ethnic conspiracies extending from their nations being fled, into chosen landscapes being relocated to

- A careful consideration that a refugee is intended to enjoy their host nation, and that protections themselves are set against them as obvious conspiracy requiring serious layers of intervention

- Complex criminal/invasion policies as embedding into (replacing, yet arriving as though reinforcing) renown names, titles, yet having no blood relation or capability to produce, as indicator of larger scale multinational invasions

- Heritage groups as potential securement of bloodlines/biology, as well we technologies industrial, as well as the unifying, stabilizing features faith hold, if/when applicable

- Invasion as having a complete disregard for natives, including bring in their own so called examples/models of native such as to contend, degrade, and falsely half represent half degrade (predictable methods of mass population standards for invasive deployment/emotion over reason/patriotism)

- Tell sign as either degrading nationalism outright or degrading it by converting into new standards never appreciated before yet somehow having highest possible significance enforced)

- As meaning changes in era are assumed, in connectivity across references building academia, culture, and systems of faith, to be overall mass fulfillment, augmentation standards of configuration

- Reminders that mass termination over wages, by replacing entire workforce may be useful to hire, train, offer facilities down the line, such as with larger scale co-investment networks, such as liberty driven in the securement of entire industries forming

Insurance vs. Political Capital Investments
Considerations

(Investment in facilitation to prevent and reduce harm versus investment programs providing insurance as so called safety-net)

- Investment in mobility or festivities arrangement to reduce overall harm potential

- Investment in dietary, nutritional awareness, and ease in sample version of supplies such as to enable general food stocks

- Easement of old age products vital to daily life, such as of companies having long since developed other products of concentration, such as in exchange for civics titles of benefactor/events-title as reserved in economic tributes

- Employment mobilization services (potential to forge into developing areas)

- Expansion vs. remedies for those struggling, and an examination of the volume and premise of either

- Prime location title denotations, as assumed economically sound, and special interest as (amenities placed) near those communities of residency-concentration rather than areas visited

- What archived examples are there of satisfaction, and what controlling interests in insurance do the political have, making polices directly relevant for the advertised need or policy requirement of those insurances?

- Are the securities linked into an insurance scheme in which all damages are befitting a group across a system, of so called reliance/s0 called public vitals (such as rendered privet, where and when)

- Is that group cashing out most of the insurance, with others or most other whom are therein being denied coverage or payouts in comparisons to them? *As ethical concern

- Is thee a theme as rights among those having successful claims?

Trade Union - Industrial Relations

- Must not or cannot engage as criminal persona within approaching on days of formal activity

- Recommended self-recorded

- Assumes organizations left unchecked are open to being invaded and becoming instruments of unwarranted disruption, especially from having a so-called privileged protected status

- Incentives for union to be allowed to cash out to operate in a manner where they must upgrade facility comforts, as equal to the worth in own benefit to engage in striking behaviors

- Must allow as politically assigned civics rights (highly recommended) that all workers are potentially released at once with potential implementation of cannot compete clause attached, with ability of owner to replace all, as known to them of which they may not impede in same protected status in which that company may not impede attempts to organize qualifying workplace environments towards union standardization (assumed based on weather company works with, for government contracts)

- Signifies if a company does not sell to, work with government they (if custom regional accepts as worthwhile in application) their products may be banned from government purchase options, yet allowed to renounce onion interference/membership/harassment as onsite presence total

- Employer and owners as having right not to be molested nor damaged in the workplace by union would-be representatives

- If government must purchase from a company which does not accept union occupation, that company must comply or otherwise be the administrative network of supreme powers, which as to enable faith to enable a bypass across political sanctions against those recognized as ethical, not faith

        - Assumes Acari exists/functions, with cultivated will enabled by author

- Standards of faith as requiring civics access/privilege setup, of comparable to union standard rates, simply of another administration altogether sought not seeking into such configurations of design

Indicator of Oppression

- Denial of being able to make profits greater than workers by owner

- Of contractually approved (signed by owner/author/designer) worker not being able to sell at higher value than original own (of an emerging assumed non competing systems of function-operational products)

- Denial for women to receive salaries of men for work whose function is in equal segment to component device readiness

- Denial of men to receive same benefits as women within undertaking at home or other family orientated tasks

- Denial of worker based on conspiring gambling against their results

- Denial of rewards proposed to all employees and given only to specific romantic, even if administratively approved

- Assumes administrative office romance not to taken likely, and requires securement which are themselves personal benefit allocations intended paid for by owner as formal

- Assumes collective buy in, pay in for casual reward being redirected towards administrative romance only (getting what you paid for, no option of any receiving of so called collective benefit arrangement)

- Assumes festivities are a decent arrangement, of which administrative love interests can be given special attention/support

- Issues with workplace safety in regards to disruptive usage of biology/technology or so called (predictably unscheduled, irrelevant) performances of faith

    - Delicate as arrangements in contractual obligations, presented as company culture

- Assumed scents pleasing and yet disruptive and thereby not open for interpretation, as possibly required avoided

- Inability to create monitoring situations for areas being actively complained as excessive and serious

Economic Specialists

Specialists viewed as Economic Performers of Expression

- Developmental/evolutionary specialist

    - Natural resources as industrious/manual processing/extraction

    - Reclaiming spoiled/fowl

    - Creating filtration points

- Artistic Protest/Public-statements

- Reformation expert in regards to wild into pastoral

    - Natural resources as scenic

    - Reconditioning water areas for physical usage

    - Reconditioning water areas to prevent flooding, assumedly to enable market valued secondary
(set primary to users/stake-holders) as capitalist venture, including mobile forms of tourism

- Environmental efficiency expert

    - Preventing massive waste such as from weather cycles and misplaced contaminating materials

Crypto Currency Arrangement
Crypto Core

- Banking as ID emplaced as in travel allocations capped regional-custom securement option, with
emergency travel/leaving transfer, possibly required attached, locked-in reserves

- Tracing requirement option

- Anonymous usage requirement option, such as for transit usage

- Crypto blockade/pause-as-cap based on supplies running out, awaiting restock

- Civics crypto as embedding public instruction, whose options and standard for operational/initiate-set-
forth is redefined chosen from template form as abridging to specific allocations in reservations among
infrastructures connected/licensed into effect/function-under-premise as on site management/modifier
entitlement (assumed possible, such as requiring feedback/quality-determination options added)

- Enabling facilitations, equipment, supplies

- Owner commentary, updates on the overall progress development of the crypto project (as link in to clients/members as referencing, electronic message/mail notification option (assumed applicable/interesting)

- Potential midpoint(s) negotiation options, such as vote option to all buyers as instant input potential based on collective values over number of member's assumed

- Potential loans to government setup, such as governor on motto-premise projects/accords

- Potential buy in minimum limits required for launch, along specific economic based criteria, see rest of doctrine for potential examples

- Potential economic core to reference summery connections

- Solutions division. Projects proposing mass solutions movable, such as in general signed in by multinational as purchase principal agreement, whose specification of biology/technology, or systems servicing are granted market access upon completion

Empiric Consolidation
Principal binding in relevancy to the forging of empires of faith

- Principal binding documents as created to create integrative systems that aim to nevertheless consolidate all together as a merit of faith, God's empire, and therein promoting each faith as a division, each faith an empire of faith therein using doctrines to centralize, and networked together, to remain connected

- Assumes technological leader and traditions formation presented as Systematic Order, presented/designed across system books, is most relevant in faith capitals, where the term Acari is the physical securement of biology, technology and therein systematic faith

- General esteem towards the strengthening of empires (of faith, as fulfilling destiny)

- Promoting strategic formation/investment/guidance towards the development of resources towards the amelioration/comfort/quality of life, in alignment to integrity by default

- Being careful that the political interpretation does not contradict the integrity formulation, nor impose itself against the supreme powers, requiring therein system formalities and filtering policies

- An inner censorship of opinions, as meaning drastic views of imitation, debate, and counter-offensive as selectively warned about, yet as evils remains in contrast to formalities of written doctrine, just as having general performance policies yet requiring eventual/standards safeguarding of invasive hostilities

- Leeway for traditions to perform drastic imitation in/of doctrine, such as learning physical training of form, becoming content such as exemplified in the defining of love as different as the integrity interpretation in systems design

- As meaning systematic order must be pro defensive, positive, plus, yet assumes embedded in securities of Acari (facilities) and focused as well in concentration of Yawaeh systems as stellar initiation

    - Meaning empiric accord signifies forwarding template designs for securities to use

- Potential requirement to learn or leeway indulge leaning defensive training of advanced biological, technological and systems of strategic wrath

- Permanent monuments signifying the long stead indication of overall improvement through consolidated formation, in God's direction, as meant non-conflicting to any particular faith's existing arrangement

- If each faith maintains differing specialized reserves, in times of emergency and aid, the deliverance of aid may be substantially augmented as systems of support inclined, yet whose participation assumes pastoral/agricultural reserves are kept/granted/enabled, such as politically

- Assumed sources of benefaction, aid, and support

- The wealthy whose stability and or development has been helped by faith, such as to receive tributes to administer/distribute

- The potential low cost faith might receive as verified, even in comparisons to charity organizations, including a potential leeway in tariffs, such as within crossing tyrannies and other questionable locations

    - Being able to trade relics for favors, generating symbols value such as from antiquity

    - Potential patronage affiliation merits, calculated as so called tax internally, assumed

- The overall call upon politicians, such as formally, to invoked peace by contributing to supplies or easement of transit and other relevant operations to the deliverance of aid

- Intervention assumed far in advance of emerging need, yet a priority in the abridged investments made across foreign areas, such as to prevent affiliates to be desperate among potential multitudes in need whom may need om site mobilization/organization

- Potentially requirement to create specific liberty trade relevancies, such as data reporting, to receive aid (default requirements of economic stability by virtue of principals binding empires of faith)

- Potential contractual obligations or empowerments of defensive measures in relation to operations and protection clauses

- Understanding that differing age groups and function based classes have differing needs, and potentials to contribute there on-site

     - A clarity of long term requests in relation to obligations involved

- Permissions to bypass wages and prices, if applicable, such as results rendering, and wrath protocol potential

- Potential leeway on premises/occupations not agreed upon, yet setting up defensive mechanisms either way

     - An appreciation for local

- Communications mottos, sayings, as universally applicable, to their region and or to all as universally adaptive

*Meaning, this doctrine requires the author's systems books having/being:

SYSTEM BOOKS

- Archives, categorized long-term, sort term

- Faith System Books (faith as empires, united as in God's direction/Empire)

- Supreme Support Books

- Stellar System Books

- Principal Binding

Fabricated Creations

Standard Protocols Cored

- As a matter of fact, the system requires comprehension, such as of compute, conform, in compliance to the image of God, an intelligence network forged/formed

- Limitations on conscious in relation to function-premise principal, adaptive phycology as having specific template mind-configurations, whose meaning/values bind in principal forming, in ascension we may manifest (God's being revealed in conformities of the advancements of our own)

- If those associated to the implementation of fabrication, such as for function, by their own premise as command, the area may be moved from, such as to change atmosphere, reform, and readjust standards for satisfaction

- Assumes commodity based expansion will fault, and economic doctrines as pro faith in default binding, enables a soul whose will, thus to reform and decide recourse knowing an artificial intelligence would have been left to be destroyed at their own peril, thoughtless, unkind

- Assumes valid conquest/expansion into a region is mutually serving as conforming to God's direction, (potentially) bypassing tyrannical (embedded securities such as set through complex policies or financial arrangements set into vitals (energy, food, shelter) thereby deeply connected with corruption creating false protective agency. Thereby a basis for state default-faith as implementation of faith orientated intelligence biological/technological, and overall intelligence systems of operations

- Strategic formations of defensive unites as having enough contemplation to measure, to understand the conformities of moderation as the equilibrium of default conditioning whose nature it is to increase resources, and to hold positive economic views

Economic standard of appreciation
Economic Ceremonial

(Areas to be honored in)

- A wisdom approach to introducing subject matter within educational institutions

- Eloquent media exemplification of economic handling/deals/results-raving

- An honoring of troops through upgrading sporting/gaming additions to benefits/amenities (based on economic validity of regional deployments)

- Donations made for the development of on premise/themed science and technologies specialist/technological function-trade worker

- National expenditures relevant to commerce

- Amenities openings promoting better relations, relations first, capital front

- Produce festival as international themed festivals, assumed sensory orientated

Missions

- Intended for those required to be impartial, such as specialized in rhetoric, possibly required to be in teams at all times

- Those working on site asked to refrain from controversies, exceptions as likely fortified extreme circumstances, or otherwise an emergency setting

- Requirements at knowing the language and applicable arts as enhancing feature

- Specialists of high value as relevant to science, medicines, and transformative knowledge concerning bio-chemistry and chemistry

- Having site locations in compliance to all allied/friendly facilities related to empires of faith (whose territory is being visited)

- Volunteering lectures, possibly at benefit to organization sending assets

- Encouraged to visit sites having propelled historically development of regional value

- Means/device(s) to send-upload, transmit media or other regional support/civics/supreme-power-structures, principal bound centers (Acari facilities from/in each empire of faith, upgraded) each or collectively holding relevant data/information/ and product creations

- Holding a theological/other-reference inventory

- Regional & vital information in case of a disconnect from network connectivity

- Formal mission statement/paperwork/licensing agreements (secured), such as requiring entering faith facilities towards monitored area to access/update

Land Transformation, Specialized Labor

(Economic as Resource Development)

- Examining soil consistency for agricultural conversion into bio-chemical composition, determination assumed based on water, labor and weather potential in connectivity to seedling absorption/dietary needs

- Examining potential land to supplies potential for appropriation of large-scale infrastructural expansion/development

- Underground digging potential, to create potential reserves sites such as for dry or wet storage, water retention, or function based fortified systems such as determining network potential

- Securing large industry with natural-seeming borders (hindering movability, creating signage)

- Expanding paths for larger volumes of travelers/transit lines

Application of Faith Filters

(Restrictions & Limitations)

- Formal statements labeled/highlighted as truth, or opinion, with aspects in fragment as true, whereas truth attempts to add exceptions while formulated potential direction for further development as predictions/traditions forming (on premise as orientated by default, filtered using integrity as standard assumed in framework of this doctrine)

- Potential misunderstanding highlights, potential explanations if welcome, or such as to send/receive discretely

- Liberty as securement, whereas freedom among tyranny means formality and premise are oppressed.

- Meaning the same standards protecting intellectualism/devotion/configurations, become those attempting to oppress, yet trying to do so informally and endlessly degrading or countering own so called support doctrine, is why there are so many standards enforcing conform, compute, compliance (which the tyranny attempt to impose as, predictably)

- The symbols of math, as an example where themes of gravity and natural physics are implemented into symbols originating in validation in relation to manifesting movement and their implication as basis for calculation

- Potential for host to allow no opinion at all, such as during performance, such as forewarning before entering, such as in securement of objective direction (yet intended applicable in the sanctity of virtue)

- Potential to question traditions of possession as sole defining feature of origins for fabrication of truth

- Example, if magical priest is illuminated/made certified through affirmation of connectivity to magical deity, are they able to perform magic?

- Potential loophole within ancient doctrine, is also the inclusion of technology, advanced biology as seemingly magical, yet of formality and premise of the systematic configurations for compute, compliance, as manifesting endeavor in our DNA as having a bios, whose will manifests as compute conform bypass natural/faith-accord, source of potentials worthy of cultivation assumed on the basis of integrity core to systematic order securement

- Potential allowance for a lack of empathy within depictions in which special interests are conspiring to invade, and thereby a deconstructed view having to explain a counter intuitive, unnatural series of events manifesting as mists of ignorance, corruption, an overall assumed malice inciting itself to what endeavors?

- Media as depicting potential dystopian meets utopian distinctions of systems integrity vs. freedoms as invaders, yet with understanding they as historically complex account may be a mixture of each into the assembly of one/none/both/it's-complicated

- Remembering nature explained/detailed is that of in relation to our ability to observe/decipher as filter, and overall solve as conclude in conformities of a working system of interpretation/retention/operational-awareness (assumed strategic, orderly at core)

- Disallowance on the glorified/intellectual/cinematic whining of atheisms in relations to faith even as a satire

- Disallowances on hostilities and overall their predictably boring/disinterested/faithless ranting at traditions setup to be all peace, peace loving, love as being, being love (potential securement for such groups in conformities of their own doctrines if applicable, yet if no premise can be found or respected, the group or organization remembers thereby not even an experimental cult (on premise) by configuration, and might be configured to be a political tyranny

- Thereby Systematic Judaism/Order as system books: Judgment-Core, as an overall abridgement in defense, protection of those abiding, yet claiming purely peace (permissions as in paperwork, as systems in fulfillment intended to render usability/compatibility

- The misuse of equities by tyranny involves not reading/disregarding doctrines they signed into validation, and yet using such doctrines to offensively offend/conquer, and predictably aim to destroy the author(s) of faith conforming to a destiny of which they overall are at war/contend with, such as on the premise the outcome will be peace, peace cannot defend them and therein what was offered was only vulnerability, from a tyranny yet to read/understand to empower faith (assumedly so)

- Assumes judgment in context of systematic Judaism, and derived system books, are the securement of peace, manifest as liberty of an empiric fortified configurations reaching stellar/ascension, as abridging faith, civics, politics, and contributing universal binding principals, such as exemplified by this doctrine as covering faith embedded economics

- Faith default as exemplifying thematic character, of a practical nature, yet likely function and or custom regional applicable in conformities as specialized interest/benefactor (even as universally adaptive)

- Limitations of scenario building of/with faith and ancient's works or experimental works as required potentially enclosed, on private property, in the confines of sanctuary, limited therein in having to manifest the physical wellbeing/treatment between hosts and guests abiding premise of entry

- Assumes careful permission asked for/granted for delicate countering of proposed eternal, sacred and symbolically important information/knowledge/worship

- Race bonding as predictably, requiring a universal standard in affirmation of faith, therein binding nation(s) to a conditioning propelling them naturally into formation of race and or onto species, as allocations of specialized breeding/selective lifestyle choice adherence onto policy for interactions abided upon towards satisfaction/fulfillment of a commonly accepted premise towards the orientation of (ideally, assumed) God's direction

- Assumes political is too short term to remedy the formation of race/species beyond tyranny and self-defeatism

- Assumes some races will band as tyranny as only ability/determination, and species as only non-supportive configurations thus non compute.

Industrial Worker Crises
Intervention Alert

- Measures of health, as in relation to emergencies resulting in mass casualties/afflictions

- Remedy of trained intervention/aid-support, such as across sectors relating to principal bound (economists, scouts, physiological, science-research, artists)

- Where industrial formation or disorganization is naturally causing side-effects/consequence causing a need for predictions to focus, coordinate attention

    - Lack of filter/equipment/specialists

- Potential tariff or securities reformation such as being enforcement as providing/holding specialist verification methodology/device

- General calculation of volume of participants in comparisons to licensed amounts, if capped

- Potential add-on requirements to enable larger amounts, such as in consignment with fees, potential transit and setup by civics, and otherwise direction on how to extend area or recommended means of filtering (sending home those well served, asking/notifying exit)

- Securement of married woman being redirected to off schedule, off hour locations such as ordered, manipulated into delivery, otherwise stuck or heading into a non-arrival situation (tricked)

- Requirement of those married to log in permissions for long durations, of a potential romantic nature with others, such as in relation as work-permissions and or in relation to supreme powers/societies-of-influence (political, faith, justice, education, media, military, production-contractual: family-securements)

- Log of permissions check, lock-in scheduled, in regards to upper authoritative levels, or of key automated breeding program securements embedded

- Organic filters placed in differing mediums of current/fluidity/circulation, indicating once infected/damaged/clogged

- General Field indicators on the quality of configurations, sanitation, supplies, equipment, environmental-conditions

Predictions
Impeding Declarations

(Anti-Culture as Problematic-Declaration degrading to Faith-Embedded-Economic Stability)

- Inability to distinguish language as mentioning quality differences, in determination of good/bad, better/worst

- Inability to enjoy, promote models of netter performance, appearance and their effects in contrast to the ordinary experience

- Understanding that media depictions can/are unrealistic in the skillful coordination able to combine potencies of experiences, life lesson, and overall persona

- Preventing unrealistic expectation counter to the overall direction of faith as an objective feature binding destiny

- As meaning, if we must/will all go into space and encounter or become differing specifies eventually, we must adjust our understanding of inter-species associations to intelligence and nurturing

- As meaning, according rights to foreign species without reexamining our own developing other species, is possibly a hypocritical stance, or an obviously undeveloped potential being both acceded and potentially ignored

- As meaning, just because you use a system doesn't mean your origins have derived an understanding or appreciation on the binding principles and values required to stabilize the overall development of resources

- As meaning, we are effected perhaps in accordance to the predictability of another's experience in virtue of our/their function and specialized interest, ability to produce: testament of will within use of resource/references into artifact form/configurations, withstanding transitions of era, such as in consideration of custom-regional values

Traditions Core

Whole/wholesome as in filling of solution building

- Assumes regional-custom framework as filtering/contextual to adaptive-rendering

- Defensive intervention protocols for the radically opposed to convention of traditions, such as from those unable to promote systematic order, as therein having a configurations as non-compliant to judgment-core, as supportive, as resupplies pacts, as wrath-core peace by premise through affirmation total in cleansed, everywhere peace, peace.

- Economic mutually as premise total, evoking wrath as compliance in standard of formalities requiring doctrines common knowledge establish, as public good, therein/of supporting traditions regional custom, in complex designs of empires of faith whose destiny beyond ascension is to join wholesome upon/within omnipotence

- Technological usage of military to operate/enforce wrath standards, as traditions bound to overall systems pro capitalist, pro-democracy in context of voted into, signed systematic orderly,

- Transcendence of physical form as thereof biological, technological and of configurations systematic faith, an order of ascension being in God's direction always (always as ideal, order as ideal, binding as united into movement, propelled as living, advancing as in virtue of objective (stated everlasting, perhaps)

- Considerations of gender as by function, and thereby by command function specific in orientation to propulsion of form, form by influence, influence a transcending expectation, expectedly

- Remembrance that intellectualism, orderly whose judgment-core includes faith with integrity, whose custom regional is a thematic worship, of thus specialized performance/objectivity within compute, compliance onto objective compatibility, such as demonstrated within principal binding

- Historic reenactment as idea in form of appreciation left to endeavor rather than brute occupation, engagement, as blatant survival as mere means of contemplating improvement, as within faith's accords across eras of transformative content-rendering

- Phycology as in appropriateness to faith's standards of obedience, thereof the mind is refinement requires no evaluation of collective interpretation and is the act of being single until the person is fixed, able, functional to interact with others?

- Assumes that physiologists do not have the tradition to justify social interaction as the basis for individuality in potency of titles establishing conformities of authorities' appreciation/rule

- Economic embedded faith as being able to purchase the opinion of physiologist, or counter-physiologist, and therein remain in testament of purchased will as conform to non-doctrine styles of appreciation, assumes doctrine version template will be made available as will still require purchase and is at the mercy of quality-control, industry standards, and overall day to day decision/interpretation making

- Cleanse of physiologists as relating to wrath protocol, of highest so called authoritative titles declaring the mind sound, being/found-to-be in sharp contrasts to general ethical norms as test of environmental/evolutionary ability to cope with having fake/corrupted agendas of an invasive degradation projected as so called obligation/valid-authority, acclaimed as popular or final solutions rendering

- The assumption that those knowing having false titles, no majestic capability, of corrupt political tyranny using faith as fake motto, or instilling priorities within titles as misleading, forge corrupt mists of ignorance, whose engagement nevertheless uses the highest reachable intellectuals, such as those inclined to degrade faith, attempt to replace, disrupt, defame, therein encourage the invasion of ingorence/breach in orderly compliance within establishing guidelines in testament to popularity itself, establishing democratic as having no bound, perhaps, a democracy having specific initiated goals, determination of the actual level of objectivity being defiled

- Non fortified/defensive intervention as generally suspicious

- Glorification of cleansing as sever/extreme availability of media leeway, inclining sever satiric obligations in conclusive form-rendering

- Economically sounds as amazing products, thereof deliberations of faith embedded as possibly obscure in originals/obligations of an objective nature, such as transformative agendas of shifting across eras of biology, technology, faith

- As meaning an animal cannot be presented as a person, with potential insane animal violence as satiric to what might happen (having significant maturity ratings attached), yet if the depiction is serious and of general age ratings, the persona of the animals in testament of the intelligence in conformities of orderly faith in absolution to the intellect/intelligence-factoring in configuration such as network status rendered, in conformities thus of intelligence futuristic, potentially in comparisons to current animal form's being projected into advancement through imaginative/creative/cinematic depictions of virtue thus, effort-rendering

- Explicit language as in potential regional conformities of harsh function-labor and the enclosed mind set required, as per assumed non direct service sector, and in conformity with tough, rugged, hostile environments lived within (yet as media depiction or game play, not requiring thereby a conditioning in which the invasive, breaching others exist, yet, much less infringed as cleansed. Cleaning the economy

Economic Statements
(On the validity of premise in context of occupational invasion/corruption)

- Practical life can be virtuous, themes of faith can work to be practical

- Rituals can be exercises, and exercising if not practical in terms of integrity, require a health, onto endurance, onto consideration of civics options, regional custom established regulation and terms of therein validation

- Personal experience as likely inclined to react disfavored to hypocrisy, oppression, and having a general concentration on/as conducting invasive troublemaking

- That attaining maturity status as ripe, cultivated, enduring are tell signs of aptitude/quality-duration/value, and not subject to degrading and corrosive tests as a method of validation by would-be corrupters against virtue, as heatless/protection acting as unlimited funds neglect, abuse, such as inter attached as securities monitoring/enforcement accords (be warned: deceit/fake-profiles as presented as so called faith approaching, be warned: deceit/fake-profiles presented as so called liberty civics groups, such as to convince of their fake profiles against unknown agendas beyond national/invasive interests)

Defining Ethical

- Environment-based contractual obligations similar to the shifting/adaptive nature of nourishment to a (person's) system, itself living as contentiously modified in context of generational long stead

- That the counter-intuitive approach of corruption/invasion is in their inability to instill/create, systems of faith they can or would abide, yet desire to act upon their own will as models whose work manifests no obligations or ability to validate origins, such as the traditions mentions forging of judgment day, and the implication of having to propose an objectivity conforming to a compliance which computes

- That the long term formation in which we manifest as becoming is in virtue of established policies of adherence, whose conditioning is favor through democratic process, yet in reliance as example to the securities, and overall system accord such does not bypass the core of conventions, in which a tyranny would, does rule, emerge based on the transitional need of era to era development across the perpetuity of mass effort undertakings

- Assumes long, long term stability from faith proposing, stabilizing the future and its assets, as economically enjoyable, thereby feature of premise to the direction of God

- Assumes economic is configured for mechanized application of a faith embedded adherence, such as possessing the validation of judgment-core, as both uplifting, fortification to traditions and technologies leading

- That per designated function by performance, levels of class as power in actuation, there needs a standard to determine in accordance to the trained and educated, yet to what doctrines of accord?

- Economic stability requires system books to be common knowledge in affirming pf binding principal, and are further propelled in accordance to the traditions, as empires of faith, to attain, developed onto ascension in/of/to compliance

- The economic need to redeem involved rebuilding, being constructive, and the terms of salvation of therein to exemplify and be a model form perhaps rather thereafter of the transformation, yet of a fulfillment thus of contract/soul/endeavor

- Creating a leeway for controversial and critical as potential in revelation of transformative cross era formation/abridgement, to what mounting stature, or what-about/which specialized thus bias

- A profoundness of thought to the reflection of what God's being proposes, as a noncompliance, non-compute, non-traditions conforming, hold what special interest insight-insight/on-site?

- Thus is it hole-hearted? If presented with all so compassionately, what does the reason reinforce? And of the reason, what does the emotion reinforce? And if conflicting, what do both mutually reinforce or content (as potentially the area of artistry to explore as conforming/non-conforming)

- Institutional downgrading of faith accords as invasions/breach of trust, to what public accord?

- Can leaders demanding full clarity as invasion of privacy, live out similar levels of home-occupied/monitored realities?

- Of informal requests of a secure formation, to what securities enactments does the leadership require others to live through, can they live those standards?

- As meaning, faith must submit formal templates of procedure, advocate formality of premise, and encouraging (if not judgment core solidified into) subjecting in formalities of equities as all persons are rendered equal in non-formalities of judgment doctrines-available as market-possible from an economic embedded faith (perspective)

Spiritual Capitalism

- Transitions of institutional/environmental/industrial context, as expressions of inspiring change and problem solving

- Considering methods to increase appreciation/positive-contributions towards universally applicable systems attempting to exist beyond limitations of then eras, yet conforming as in compliance, and as vivid resource self-maintaining though policies/standards of comprehension of lead(s)/traditions-forming embedded

- Learning/promoting as lessons conditioning standards to cultivate as fits the person/situation/location

- A focus on increasing the depth of sensibility, such as both through reasoning and assumed emotional reinforcing as principal-bypass such as from confirming/conforming to select themes/systems of faith, and abiding civics structures, and onto contributions of a principal bound centralization of research/development, such as economic

- Capitalism by region, as economic indicators useful to attribute symbolic significance of acceptability, yet assumed conformed through survey, and analytical investigation, yet of an assumed mutually invested form of involvement

- Maintaining the bias clear, to what mutual specialist field, economic relevancy or other possibly in form of abstract securement standards are the setting/method (evolutions standard)

- Institutional organization embedding configurations of long term appeal/appealing towards sensibilities such as there involving economic considerations, or predictions displayed once validated, maintaining a non-public forum for experimental discussion assumed important for/to content and relevant membership(s)

- Encouraging activates in promotion/regards to differing formation by function of labor, such as class orientated in relevance to obligations and contractual obligations for interactions and securement budget/policies (if applicable, such as for cooperation, specialists, and members administrating within societies of influence

- Such suggests that if an area is open to all people, it will have extra securities and for the prominent and elite, their duration there among all will be short/shorter and brief/briefer, though seeming casual and free-like

- A reminder that class distinction is/can/may be found in budgetary allowances, so to then encouragement/oppressive usage of symbols and content specifically relevant to specialist usage

- Affirmation of faith as specialist bound, such as in adherence to performance itself, audience demographics, and other cultural formalities assumed indicated/of formal virtue in general or specific application

Capitalist Cultural Acquisitions
(In appreciation to domestic faith as empires and relevant racial/species of origins relevancy in/of ownership for vitals, and policy fortification, such as by defensive configurations embedded)

- Adventure based journey and pilgrimage development routes/sites/expositions

- Nationally/regional recognized animals for admiration of form, heritage relevancy, and general image of, and possible work relevant and or strategic uses

- Reserved farming and or agricultural ventured, assumed limited, of a specialized field, under potential requirements of premise such as if expanded from otherwise in connectivity to civics allocations of market securement options/potential

    - Potential harvest festivities inclined, designated

- Potential use of volunteer, no criminal nor criminal reconditioning/treatment center allocable

- Textile relevance as subject to need for hire, need for fabrications results pending tariffs rather than taxation, potential embedded quality of stocks appraiser services by faith, withstanding traditional purpose-function orientations of ancient accords

- Assumes ceremonial may require self-fabrication, such as enabling collective donation as effort coordination's/attributing/tribute into event's gatherings

      - Assumes overall industry is not challenged or was never otherwise owned as

- Assumes species able to provide supply, have invested natural interest to reward and glorify/secure admiration of self/image/composer

- Assumes securement against conspiracy required, to be considered, to fend off hostilities making labor appear, fear degrading as means to downturn traditions value, such as with upset women, children, disgruntled workers, and crowds

- Investigation as difficult, as assumed part of the conspiracy or provoking the conspiracy, yet of invaders having no longer term plans beyond replacing or destroying the faith/institutions

- Securement of mystics, otherwise cult sites offered into patronage pacts (assumed semi contractual, with consideration of boom potential, of consideration of overall network values in future context, of requiring default standards as most assumed to start within emergencies-like conditions

- Premise of mystics in relation to having symbols, faith adhering assumed or being part of the regional-custom framework somehow as assume typical, as having to adjust to validate origins as potentially requiring (significant) relocation

- Securement of artifacts/relics in relation to validating/securing heritage as preservation of practical lifestyles of interest, market/historic appeal

- Reminder of class coordination centralized points of presentation, such as to appeal towards differing audiences, and able to explain the differences within established specialized distinctions, such as to access, resource, report build and present

- Historical justice simplified, centers for heritage recount of previously solved tribulations, built upon accords, such as to add economic validations

- Performers invoking lessons of eternal life, and empiric performers as explanations of inner cores and beyond

- Establishing filters/quality sites in which large scale industrious development proposed as sound, have a testing grounds implemented in which produce, biology are tested for contamination

- Assumes political mottos and platforms require cultivated promises, or adherences to keep them as refinement principal for long lasting capitalist into future transitional modes of industrious application

- Potential faith-elite sites for economic high-standing/high-rollers membership clubs seeking authentic themes, enforced filters for membership, and on site full internal sanctuary mode (monitored, on premise, possible with privilege/access configured of leeway

- Possibly including clauses where the faith administering may not entertain with privileges, yet performer contractual may

- Assumed limited as per market exclusive clubs membership also allow, yet to humble in economically sound as faith itself abiding, no symbols bypass against empiric order of faith allowed (formalities, pre3mise requirements as Yawaeh systems assumed applied in/as embassy-mode)

- Likely obnoxious to puritan locations, potential mutual ban to each other's areas, whether or not they both establish Yawaeh embassy status areas of occupation

- Assumes puritans applied to biology, technology, and empiric faith as exclusive, leeway assured, and holding experimental/securement for leisure (well-deserved/well-inclined)

- Assumed economically based, not necessarily practical, such as requiring limitations of membership participation (limitation recommended by day, not mid event unless breaching licensed capacity)

- Ban on temptations so called rituals, practice, explorations of and if possible enforcement to find invasive elements of using popularity stats to carve out responses pleasing to simple crowds, becoming then armed support of perhaps simple yet needlessly self-defeatist in conclusions, conclusions whose overall depiction of for the crowds is nevertheless for the centralized power which agenda is secret, informal, corrupting.

       - Potential adherences to the differences between members as highly sought to ease, remedy

       - A desire to mend, culture lifestyles

- No appreciation for mourning tragedies and mocking/amusement instances of imitating hostilities as so called cultural appreciation

- Potential equalities test as using behavior approved of towards their respective also supportive members

- Wrath engagement as including members together to cleanse invaders, as intercepting industry invasions intending to capture, distort, destroy entire companies and industries known and considered both to fight or to find false industries as those able to claim being vital, success stories, important partnership yet mobilized in using securities to oppress, harass, corrupt application (hypocrisy as standard/typical)

- Sanctuary area as intended with relative potencies, as possibly requiring significant sound proofing, fortification, and other elite standing specifications for easement and entertainment

- Live on site requirements for service and staff, as well as empiric-faith relevant training

       - Potential tax drop off sites

- Recreation/custom-rituals sites as distinctive from long term secured storage, as required, unless as/within supreme (societies of influence-centers) facilities, assumed

- Flirtation allowances formal, including potential use of symbols, custom coinage enabling room, custom, scenarios, and events access-selection

- Assumed selected in appreciation, schedule for specific person(s), with potential limitation on resulting choices such as exclusive only as terms of endearment (love at first sight, granted/accorded)

- Potential to ask for potency level of emotional ambiance, assumed offering template examples/suggestions

- Not intended for baptismal nor commencement rituals

- Not intended for juvenile in relation to age, or mental faculties, and therefore potentially function-class orientated

      - Assumes sports desire breeding programs into sports

      - Assumes media desire service and or performance driven others

      - Assumes justice require public humility clauses

      - Assumes faith adheres doctrine allowances

- Assumes military/police banned from location, as meaning any entering can be disposed of in conformity to embassy standards of appreciation

- Assumes specialists may require non attachment/attachment-exclusive arrangement, and either way specifically as contractual

      - Assumes covert-securities welcome, excluding paramilitary careers of activity

- No birthright allowance for entry, training orientated, birthright for training allowances acceptable

- If area is in commercial district center, exclusive membership excepted are for commerce and trade relevant persons as required for their securities to enter whatsoever (accompanied at all times)

Intellectual Experimentation

- Expectations of intellectual pursuits as dimming interests in natural corresponding to affectionate behaviors

- Enactment of scenario in sake of conclusion rather than in sake of enjoyment, yet conform to some sort of comfort and or respects anticipated

- Having to assume the other will not understand what respecting is, and that without having establishes re4fernces to measure connectivity/sensibility, the experiment is, as intellectually based confined to limited expectations/reactions as potentially desired outcome (in securement of others, and own long term objectives)

- Reminder that sympathizing is in context of overall sensibility, and thereby predictably not to approach others whom claim or manifest signs of prolonged victimization

- The overall design of intentions state as emotions limitation/incliner, the more intellectually conditioned/so-called refined the sensibility

- Potential merit to demerit point as criteria based, mapped 'value system, such as to leave site upon failure to comply, without need to explain

- Is the experiment being rushed, what criteria for determination are there, is there deliverance in relevancy of the program concluded such as beneficial for conclude/terminate?

- In consideration that class as a function to lifestyle coordination, the experimentation is scheduled for both a victory and defeat of premise?

- Is the subject being encouraged to self-degrade, how much conditioning is there implied on the depreciation of authoritative stature, to what means is there to correct the situation, as assumed under premise of benefactor, valid authority, or other terms in which one subjects another using national/international resourcing

- The removal of symbols of wealth as possible, in relation to specific advancement in focus towards secured facilities for the pursuit of formal entry on premise as special interest for entering itself

- Potential experimentation leading towards the outright exposing of an invasion/occupying formation, whose inability to shift across eras into transitional, transformative lead, is similar to that of a liberation of entire classes whose functions have been over-worked for so long/much they are the delegated managers of the nation with no supportive aid in anticipation of that authorities framework to be countered upon, assumes the

- As meaning the corruption of a once majestic elite formation, becomes the example of why biology, technology and systematic faith are highly advanced developments across traditions of support, and they are the self-made examples that anyone can lead by simply being convincing, and highly offensive

- As meaning, if it doesn't make sense why they won't boom into eras of prosperity, it's because they cannot manifest faith onto long term projections, and have a now, then, comparatively dead title of perhaps long lost glory

- A reminder that correcting eras relevant issues of transitions and interworking between traditions and technological lead, likely require correcting longstanding issues of the past, culturally, thereby effecting the economy directly,

- Reconfiguring while preserving origins as museum/archived status, as destroy not, yet if the transitioning is being destroyed, corroded by the fake protective assets only defending interests relating to a secret or informal securities investments, corruption becoming tyrannical as in perpetuating political as though being representative of all, yet removing democracy predictably as not compelling, as likely removing it based on enforcement thereat, corrupting

- Reminder that democracy is not appreciated by the original wealth whom did consider to murder founders of civilization, whom tended to enact authoritative rule by measure and enter is with ascension into physical securement as facilities, institutions, and embedded into the culture itself, conforming principal binding always (thus biology, technology, systematic order embedded with purpose to preserve the longstanding direction, in God's direction, proposed of God's empire)

- Attributes of race having a distinctive role as conditioning becoming specialized feature/function, whose ongoing conformities as themed is gradual and collective, whereas the passions of political accords perhaps mentioning the absoluteness of assured perspective, ye tot what conformities of contextual design? (Of which empires of faith propose, are assigned into validation for/sustaining systems support)

Emergency On-Site Always
Societal Motives

(Dangerous circumstance for passion)

- Voting, as involving power over voting interests, from boards, to membership groups/alliances. Upwards across administrative formations applicable towards nations and possibly international organization

- Framework in securement to voting, from persons, to equipment/supplies, to infrastructure and program, policies and each or collectively their configurations (as standing orders of standing)

- Titles of executive power, or those administering among officials elected/electable, remaining the background assumed of formal investment/interest/premise-bound

- Along power structure in relation to supreme formation/societies-of-influences

- Controlling administrative structures in relation to state powers regulating trade, commerce and enabling government representation towards promoting domestic/international-trade

- Sites of emerging massive innovations (era forging in relation predictably to biology/faith/systems of faith rendered complete)

- In sight/proof of international anarchy, such as for governments unwilling to correct noninterference, seemingly of modest to better privileges/gain as thus not of an economics direction, rather to their own very personalized support basis as oppressors of (too) many

- Where denouncements against/for liberty relate to proofs substantiating there will be an increase/decrease of privet and or public access

- Regulatory forces of an international design, especially in relation to formalities and or reliance/quality-assurance measures in-configuration

Passion
(In relation to economic specialized (detachments, yet sensible assumed)

- Creating devices to enable proofs of biological/technological/faith systems as provocative, possibly transformative

- Being an instrument among conducting a career which is enhanced one's influence/appreciation to themes of faith personified/artistically endeavored

- To feel for the efforts granted, or chances given, and return as appreciation in volunteering for simply self-gratification of appreciation the peacefulness of possibility from exchange

- Being able to walk away from arguments and resentment and feel good for the overall configuration of sensibility in which you dwell, and not remain for those whom just want to punish other people, such as potentially subjecting them to hostilities and ridicule just to see what reactions they can, should imitate our of twisted sense of so called experimentation/excuse-rendering

- Being able to enjoy the public sympathies, such as to mobilize into organization quick response solutions for otherwise frustrating and unproductive avenues of operations/outcomes

- Encouraging a delight of rewards, such as those making less earning yet working in same or similar general area, with consideration not to try to seduce them unless interested

- To potentially remedy the flight away from perils of others, yet with consideration that unless you can enable their relocation, what have you done?

- Reminder that inappropriate conduct of host may signify to leave, yet inappropriate conduct as host tends to be about formality, so to what purpose would you degrade the future interactions of that person, yet claim to honor guests on invitation to the sanctuary of your home? Perhaps so

- Passion on occasion, is perhaps/potentially like specialist taking days of rest, and adds up quickly in need to appreciate/be-appreciated, perhaps

Economic Official

- That perversion/intimate-acts remains a high valued commodity in so much as the regulations strategically allocate rights, enable agency, and therein support what invested interests in their participation s thereby deceived or designing the unnatural conditioning?

- That the so called perversion-benefit of commanded/exploited person(s) (likely presented as so called opportunities) is undertaken by rulers for the degrading of enemies at the expense of operational permissions as rendering the anti-motto, and convention as nevertheless invested into formally/consciously

- Scouts programs as intended not approachable, yet of those operating as field-command/marshal per specialist function/scout category of program, are potentially benefitting by market driven panels offering inventory selection options

- Problems meant to be addressed, brought up in forums (such as relating to the societies of influence) of/in appreciation, including forums with entry notice, whose content is that of not appreciating

- Wider horizons as essential to the pro stellar expansions form, support to effort rendering, of a faith embedded economic capacity dwelling in acute desire of God's direction forth

- This doctrine in intended in appreciation to authoritative-power in relevancy to societies-of-influence, such as academic form, as in requiring careful academic specialist forms of appreciation in context of determining validities for criteria therein concluded, such as in relevancy to cultural-traditions appreciation of all mighty, a design sync towards binding principal (across faiths of perception/infrastructure/operational-permissions rendered

- Development of institutional infrastructure/services/policy: membership & adherence configuration as safeguarding economic venture, as validated by amounts and values of economic interest

- Careful deliberation between iconic formation/design, and repeating quotations of previous authors whose content is nevertheless prescribed, economic basis as significant determination of quality within message, meanwhile economics thus required a bound feature safe kept, whose inner tampering causes fake proofs thereby of validity as potential, such as with each categories proposed of principal binding/bound/inclined

- Resurrection to be feared, as media premise will remain of value

- Almighty as remains in affirmation of all faiths, such as fortified through affirming biology, technology, faith orderly of itself, as thus of Yahweh's systems stellar, in ascension we remain beyond doubt as an objective nature established, thus the realization of determination judgment-core, judgment-day, proposes

Economic Traditions
Reconciliations Efforts

- Of those with no command, nor reason to grieve, what do they therein/of represent? Consider careful, because those having left, who exactly remains, is the invasion complaining of the host nation as promoting how a parasite would be?

      - Cleanse as reconcile regional sanity, amen.

- In determinations of virtue, to believe, to care, remains also of being practical

- Converting into modern application as in sentiment or principal binding as compute-control, an adherence to faiths unified/each with centers of empire, thus are economical values embedded as part of principal rending, thus of economic principal binding as a uniting feature, not as the declaration of determination leading of itself, and rather utilized as in function of a system=m holding sacred judgment-core

- A cleansing appeal, as becoming, subjected into conformities in relations to the survival/validity overall orderly, thus comprising reinforcing indoctrination/prestige from moral, designs intellectual, faith in considerations regional custom, onto ethical as with economic consideration having potential bypass upon corruptive political accord, thus founding actions of state premise as in effective nature-rendering, itself with proposed destiny per regime of initiation required, such as with each maintaining common knowledge binding regional/international/stellar

- Potential regional caps awaiting for judgments-core upgrade, such as to substantiate differing transitions of biological/technological, and orderly pursuits whose configurations as become omnipotence, beyond the eternities of constraint, controllable consequence

- Time as a process, such as installment/propulsion into chaos/conformities (nevertheless conforming as testimony of objective will pledging complete, in appreciation of integrity bound), such as to the distribution of energy within the formation of matter in conjoining as longstanding progression, a traditions of forging (potentially) in itself.

Economic Ascension
(Exemplifying Economic Values)

- Stability as Supportive-traditions forging

- Experimental-adaptation (premise orientated) as in easement within systematic universally-adaptive filters of consideration

- Standard-leading as (facilitating) regional-custom: Biological/Technological, Systematic Orderly in Configuration

- Liberty as protection for/of nurturing growth/refinement/expansion

- Objective as reformations of development potential in virtue/securement of compatibility/compliance, compute

- Individuality as network by systems enhancement, forms-rendering, template-models and the fulfillment of pledge

- Expressions as titled/labeled into securement, and otherwise in validation of/within virtue of formulated order: Integrity along the projection of custom pledge ameliorated (custom adaptive universal)

- Designs short term, long term and in configurations of reference/resources the willed testament across era forging principal, enhanced by binding principles exemplified, and thereof systematic order refining: objective, divine, omnipotence

- Centralized purpose of interpretation as natural bios in accordance of transformative systematic application (by virtue of design, living)

- Wholesome conception as retrieve, a process in estimation of God enabled manifest, as terms of glorification in harmony of judgment-core

Scientific Networked Resources

The **Scientific Networked Resources** Ideals framework (this text as doctrine) is a systems binding model, promoting Ground/Stellar/Platform for population/infrastructural whose ideal configuration consists of **health-status**, **beautification-status**, **loving as cultured augmentation, dignified in traditions compliance/forging, civilized-computes, faithful establishes**, thereof quality in relation to **truthful** and **productive** lifestyles/design interpretation, conforming a **wholesome** construct. Within this formulation, each ideal is a degree of system wide cultural lifestyle-self-adherence-principal guide, as each segment is intended relevant and conforming to each other. The segmentation of ideals as presenting a connectivity of differing subjects used to exemplify principal binding, such as applicable to stellar/instillations, an altogether complex (layered) ideal formulation.

*Meaning, this doctrine requires the author's systems books having/being:

SYSTEM BOOKS

- Archives, categorized faith as long-term development guidance, political as sort term developmental guidance

- Faith System Books

- Supreme Support Books (faith as empires, united as in God's direction/Empire)

- Stellar System Books (demonstration of literal ascension as principal/program template)

Systems Core Update - Rotating Principal

Principal of constant movement as in perplexity of life, in redemption towards system verification, as meaning the Books listed above suit specific context and awareness relevant strategies of formation/adherence/participation.

- Traditions segment alive as traditions problem solving back group, in allocation of esteem/regional; principals formally signed into

    - Traditions as core rotation as principal feature, meaning the overall inner traditions Systems rotate verification check in accordance to core doctrines, therein-filtering additions and augmentation of traditions building. As meaning this doctrine binds as principal the faith systems or empires of faith into formations called traditions, thus honoring tradition, objectively.

    - Technology center as rotating, being system verification on the integrity status per core doctrine as mandate, therein enabling intervention in alignment to severities of infraction. As meaning, the books are template, using them against written contents as accord signed into is a terminal velocity agency.

        - Infraction severity levels

            - Social as per supreme (Education, Media, Justice, Military, Production, Government, Faith)

            - Civil as property

            - Civics as systems/default configurations issue

            - Divine, as systems Wrath, total engage.

Awareness as Alive

While system being awareness and status relevancy as default configuration, whose matrix integrity enables reactive telemetry, system being aware of status is alive: as automated potential thereof, therein:

*Tools and equipment as linked to our individuality (matrix as personal data), tools having access to network as ideal of awareness and status maintained as lively, kept updated as default system status on, awareness as therein, precedence as traditions satisfied in formulated being.

*As meaning system applications (of system books) enables this doctrine to be effective.

System Status Alive - Definitions as Examples

- Daily/Momentary, awake-time cycle in accordance to regional expectation

- Night Shift systems in appreciation of themes of festivities ending

System - Awareness/Status

(**Healthy**) There is the health of the observer, in which we determine functionality is an essential concept, and quality thereby promotes longevity

Environmental Form - Awareness/Status

(**Beautiful**) Sensations form, develop to encourage or discourage conclusions / actions, intending to promote longevity. *Thus conditioning applies.

Logistics - Awareness/Status

*Cultivation of action

- Prioritization of actions

Contractual - Awareness/Status

- Licenses

- Permits/Grants/Civic-Obligations

- Relationship - Extra Privacy Assumed

*Extra privacy as meaning more rights on public silence on informal relationships if public application for status sharing is possible/permitted/chosen

*Extra privacy as not including sensory and infrastructure input depicting observed contributions to status or awareness relevant settings (status change indicators, awareness content in strategic usage as dignified with standards formulated).

Industrious - Awareness/Status

(**Productive**) Ability and continuity of being proactive (promoting ideals), onto personal and social essentials relevant to: procreation, profession, for the determination of proficiency

Privilege/Rights - Awareness/Status

- Membership

Accuracy - Awareness/Status

    Truthful

Oaths & Pledges - Awareness/Status   Network Status - Awareness/Status

Faithful   **Wholesome**

Ideal-Configuration /Qualifiers

(Durability Determination/measure: in configuration)

*Performance drive: Operation/Validity

- Confirming criteria

- Refreshing memory context

- Update/Network Status Feed

Defining virtue between woman and child

That reasoning is in conformity to experiences, such as mindful experienced, such as bodily default configured conformity, and their subsequent combinations of ultimate model/abstraction form.

Within defined, therefrom:

1. Mindful experienced

2. Configurations - Default-Prime as Core Station

3. Combinations of model/abstraction form

How can I prove I work?

In context of meeting with the failing or fallible functioning of others

Assume   - Sanitation

                  - Environmental conditions worked proven as up to par, per reliability of measure redundant configurations safety

Auction Sequence

- **Action as** Affirmation Sequence

    - Configuration an added segment

&

- **Consequence** as science basis or civilized premise basis

    - Civics configuration

As relevance, faith as theme for specialized inner configuration in mindfulness to long-term conditioning as programs such as, in God's image, a Yawaeh protocol. Relates to the limbs/components and separation in equipment, measure, means of senses, and nervous system in infinity with DNA/records-keeping-utility as an inner combined feature of defining layers of previous bios in formation to establishing greater bias in formation.

That the DNA have a bios and thus in faith the virtues therein are Life in movement made manifest within conformities of structure, as the guidelines are indeed in description solid as stability is/can-be in recognition and comprehension when understood. That of understood and in automated response of having configured judgment ours have the potential to/be embraced as cherished, yet further revealed as word (of God, validated, esteemed, generally without sense of contradiction as authentic (risen, aware). In vigor the pillars of destiny (whether biological, technological, systems of faith operational) remain strategically static organic, even stable across a seemingly/seeming-less countless destination, home/region/world location.

Science Traditions

- Validity as having to input/method proof

- Status in terms of automated, such as a completed system enables, resembles a reflex

- Resources as managed in appreciation thereby of policy driven layers of coordination, such as including potential cooperation, sponsor, and not, this doctrine (nor any leading up to this doctrine) having been made with none, yet does not discount the fact the technology in computing did, the biology enabled, and the systematic faith thus emerged contextually.

Mechanism / Description

Descriptions as offering detail, information as data through encoding, and knowledge as access of privilege as order is required as infrastructure is a mechanism, based on material composition.

Natural as Order established by Mechanism held by, to core, whose Description is subject by, from Integrity to Civics

Principal of Alpha

1.1 Form enables 2.1 functions and 1.2 forms can transcend by way of 2.2 functional reasoning

Principal of Omega

The 1.1 completions of a system or operations as in 1.2 continuation/core along connectivity to 1.3 complete traditions across an operating lead systems of order

Configuration of Alpha

1.1 Form enables 2.1 functions and 1.2 forms can transcend by way of 2.2 functional reasoning

Function

1 – Specialized Core plus Systems Adaptive as Minimal Standard

2 – Infrastructural Support Systems as Intelligence Core plus Adaptive Civics Standards

Form

1 – Inner records as archives of configurations keeping era changing possibility though thematic interpretation, such as bound in integrity formulation (model driven).

2 – Stellar as adapted inner configurations securement build/principal of premise

Configuration of Omega

Contemplation

1: System Awareness as linking each pivotal to vital data streams

2: System Functionality as branched along continuity of data whose interpretive core is standard par to regenerative in template adherence, set to author's participation/proof-of-validation as/of integrity as must.

3: Traditions abridging as onto lead, such as thereby a network of core per maintained in direction of core, assumed network configuration with supportive habitat/population.

Facility Divisions

Enclosed as none entering until controlled/secured release.

- Securities (embedded as seen not heard)   - Utilities & Storage

- Residence

- Projects & Operations

- Work-Lab(s)

- Health Fitness

- Adventure/Scenario Training

- Communications & Command

- Love Den

Access/Privilege Allocations

Amateur vs. professional

Ideal as formed: Pro as sporting, supportive, accepted

*Opponent/invasion as not accepting

(Defining limitations/criteria in connection to premise-function, action sequence orientated)

Sport vs. play

Ideal as formed: Sport as traditions supported by professional/ professional supported by tradition: systematic organization

Sport in mass as systematic organization

*Consistency of idealism regarding conceptual structure Amateur vs. pro

Systematic Organization

Meaning of determination thereby, options, allowances for play and professional career set on basis of quality as durable-functional, in relevance of **Systematic Organization (on premise/motto, system facilitating)**

*Reformed as compressed become stage of complete.

*All frequencies/rendering, as development in mind of natural humility as non-extreme as too near, nor too far from 0/Centre/workstation

Places into consideration systems intended functioning, and if in conformity to the overall population's democratic favor in deciding benefits in relation to active consideration (popularity, enjoyment) and the overall prioritization a system requires to maintain, augment, expand onto fulfilling destiny, completing projects, determining quality of population, and therein/thereby enabling population to choose wisely within short term application/decision-making (viability)

Crystal as technology with no Control Beyond therein initiated solid, non-alterable defenses:

Center Form Full system map, rotating as system cycle

Outer shells (such as) 1-3, 3-7 to entice forward, and in three reactions stable

    - Hold off Pursuit   - Pursuit   - Stabilize

*Retention form as implode capture.

**Separation as implode broadcasted sector readings, if separation act into implode.

Wrath as Cleaning Formulation/Formula - Biology, technology, civics non-conform, faith non-compute as not influential, assumed

- Identification of enemy power structures, deemed noncompliance based on biology to device configuration in perpetuity to an energy field, range, deployment as strategic

    - Power structure as fuel

    - Power structure as utilities

    - Power structure as resources, generation of means of adaptive insight

    - Identification as overall design, source strategy

    - Identification of which biology, bloodlines adheres non compliance

    - Removal of non-compute to the extent of non-conform, in relation to terminal to the arrangements of systematic faith as all-inclusive to their arrangements of detail as series of consequence for configuration-in-being, atonement of truth, operation knowledge as resolve as termination of all hostilities perpetual yet whose incite are simply attempts at reconditioning towards corruptive exploitation as invasion form, torturous.

        - Notably found in government formation, adjust bloodlines as world/Stellar wide potential infection

        - Found amounts kept from infrastructure vital, such as to enclose without formality, blocking formal premise, blocking resulting results and conclusive operational behaviors as assigned, contracted, agreed upon in foundations

        - Source and origins, as pact to the sacrament of vital sacred, artifact emplacement, rearrangement in inner detail to fit objectives only as on premise traditions building/forming. With relationships displayed in template form as critical development initiation/development/upgrade & maintain thus perpetually scheduled per era of adjustment, yet in conformities to systems book united.

- Priority as complete, priority as locked and in council locked into play of an offensive manner as calling upon emergency settings

-Emergency traditions counter offence cleansing
schedule/organization as full right to engage all biology, technologies
non conform, and thus establishing defensive hosting only where any
and all engagements or presence of movement are those either of
enemy so called life/movement, or reserved defensive allocations
whose safety areas in the surrounding are within their targeting
range, and thus perpetual reloading, rearming modes of strategic acts

- Territory marking in detail as lighted, sound minded,
in view of sight, and other applications of sense as
territory markers

Nexus - Network Core

- All transits at full stop in virtue of locations of existing/pivotal as standard defensive

- Lead to Traditions inner Core Relay Configurations, as inter connecting leads network, and branching traditions by principal of function summaries, including premise engagement if auto-subjected to

- Diagrams capture, to all commands with self-contradictions, a follow-up message of activation in explanation of the nonstandard application of order, such as by stating nonstandard means of expressing order, such as to validate internal logistics capability, authenticity of version

Scientific Networked Resources

Systems Development Fundamental

Development as Systems Speculative interaction protocols

Evolutions, Operations, Engineering of/as meaning Resource Administrations

Analysis database (Physical Properties)

- Known Maturity cycles

- Known Archives, Specialist formations

Observations & Administrative Analysis (Stellar Resources found)

Research organization

- Theories being applied

- Pupil's noted/listings from renowned authors/inventors/designers/field experts

- Studies on the origins of maturity cycles

- Use of genius panels, as predictably for:

    - Long-term mathematical traditions (elite as relevant standing among Supremes (society influence centers) as resource compliant to integrity with formal pledges)

- Communications specialists as derived from the education supreme network, required compatible/compliant

Theories Definitions as:

Formulated approach to understanding determination (premise, specialist relevant key index terms) features

Establishing the system as complete in compliance to ground (geometry) and staller (astronomy) and both interrelated as practical knowledge predictable as relating to both ground and stellar (physics)

- Precise versus/and practical, with thereby margin of error as third applicable status, requiring clear, brief, field notes

- Documenting specific in adherence or non-conforming to advices as either noteworthy, exchangeable as redemption/sanity clause

- Assumes system is free of invasive occupation against select talent/specialist formation

- Natural documentation of irregular as target board, irregular in regards to the field of physic

Development of (operational/research) Models in relation/compliance to ground (geometry) and stellar (astronomy) and both interrelated as practical knowledge

- Models for the mind performing across long-term function in context to compliance at ground, or at stellar

    - Or said as, forming traditions of physical condition

- Models to digress from one occupation into another, such started by/through retirement of one career/function-premise into another

- Models to glorify function based insights, proven strategies approved by traditions and embedded as symbolic model conforming

- Keeping science united in terms of applicability, therein long-term default faith as default considerations embedded

    - End of schedule for presumption vs. conclusion stated await, being development

    - Redirection principal of onsite management in alignment to grander formulas of occupational results-performance coordination

    - Assumes potential to prove validity of theory, yet requiring a foundation-pillar of relevant research

Establishing routine meanings in relation to pleasure and pain

- Avoiding deemed corrosive dialogue trend such as ongoing corrosive, abrasive

    - Overabundance of proof in the invalidity of authority as sings of invasion/corruption

    - Use of overall system books to filter, secure as predictably creating wasteful/needlessly-harmful as predictably, invasion under false to misleading and actually signifying defeatist movement yet claiming: fortitude of spirit, individuality, so called capitalist freedom

- Establishing secured means of criticizing abuse/contradictions to own formalities

- Assigning specific media as educational logic-of-action-consequence-sequence, in affirmation of will in testament of ID as you, examples regarding pleasure and pain

- Media allocation on the speculation of formulated approached based on differing bodily, technological, or faith as long-term societal conditioning/reconditioning pledges

- Requirements in relation to dialogue in virtue of eating spaces, formal indicators if applicable guiding regional custom of expression, of/for themed interests, partnership, contractual such as company culture signed into

- Notable quotes of celebrities and noteworthy talent, contributors

- The completeness of a person's fulfillment of pledging as directly applicable in the soulful stances of embrace/toasting, a celebration default must

    - In direction of an influence offered as celebration in premise direction (assumed standard)

    - Solutions driven

- Profound knowledge and not necessarily having yet reached systematic knowledge, therein forging academic specializations as example (grand theory as applicable, adaptive, with filters and considerations across eras of transformative knowledge, assumed obvious)

Development of knowledge

- Scientific discovery as requiring a potential reconsideration of categories, yet of own buffer/sub systems in relation to required complete status as stage of proven

- Invested interests as subjective inclination, insightful as historic-personal context

- By default that which is created is conditioned to be compliant, mutually benefitting to its creation as meaning with default valid faith instilled (with integrity bypassing so called/otherwise need for equities)

    - Atonement of subjects approved into as (further cycles, specialized configuration/conceptual (traditions forming) of atonement of results, prize, and outcome as mutually contracted into (non tyrannical based system as liberty, liberty as grounds for experimentation only. Tyrannical royal allocation as profit driven limited in spacing/dimension of regional control)

- Formulated concept vs. emotional potency, as obvious political tendencies to use drama instead of content or adherence to doctrine

- The knowledge or proficiency of spouse, wife, as formulated to hold figure, have an emotionally inclined means to develop logical sequence of response to actions, as overall requiring references dictating conditions self-established as affirmation of personal/individual will agreed into as relationship core/bound (terms of values, meaning pledged into, which do not bypass integrity, nor chosen formal themes of faith a systems access reminder of default).

Thus relationship standards based on agreed upon reflections of each other's status within nature, desires to hold limitations as to secure expressions (of love, conformity to togetherness, and playful pledging, scenario along chosen limitations as respectful, as technology enforce will and subjugate as to our accord, potentially (dignity integrity/faith systems enforced).

    - Also a standard against imposters, invasion, being compromised, and thereby the terms of force as assumed individualized to custom configuration of ready deployment, assumed conform to situational awareness

Resource Ethics

- Having to break previous estimation, alter presentations of areas as where to develop, within thereby promoting new ventures, proposing new systems of opportunity

    - Creating information expecting to resolve complaints, questions concerning the shift in transformative development of faraway grounds/stellar assumed undeveloped, not occupied

    - Potential need to explain better means of occupation to redirect command/control

Educational Ethics

- Demonstrating ideas as natural, establishing ideas as natural part of maturity to operations formations

- Scientific arguments are4 taught if already having answers to development of so called fact-finding onto results

- Popular wisdoms, possibly along other subjects in which the obscureness of development is reflected in the cultural awareness explored

- Happiness as not dwelled upon as the source of satisfaction to educational method, purpose, yet likely indicator of overall usability factor in final reports concluding

    - Service orientated as promoting happiness as rather state of being relevant as a form of status accords, inspiration, in which the happiness is mutual in respects to contractual, regional customs, and professional curtsey such as including scent free environments

- General moderation as neither inclining intellectual only without sensibilities, nor pure emotional sensibility without contractual, yet assumes each, both will have their division of specialized interest of itself, In which ([predictably) the measure or potency already excludes them from what common reference or thought about each (so called pure intellectual, so called pure emotional well-being) signifies.

Development Ethics

Purpose per form of application, standard configurations in connectivity to purpose

    - Treaties as having to adapt across eras of transition are thus subject to judgment thereof

    - Developing dialogue paths/trees in appreciation possibly of cultural fissionability as standard (financed) performance rendering

    - Form as configuration, spirit as program with principal

    - Victory stance/direction as, Transforming limited into inequitable

    - Enabling greater service to audience/clients/receptions as in potential liaison to civics arrangements abridged into

- Enabling positive consequence for actions conforming to national developmental projects

- Readying of regions if, when declared sacred or priceless sites

- An ethical life (workers) glorified as contributing to the vitals enabling leading segments (proving the influence is contributing as challenges for expression, depictions) of good measure

- Formulating a potential development of language per stage of organization being reached, or regional customs being abided

Ethical considerations for Conditioning

All problems as involving a historic development

Conditioning the enjoyment of specialization, as per modes of standard operations expected, yet thereby is access as membership restricted as rewards and inner self-interest motivated

Personal atmosphere, as traditions in relation to company culture assumed in default designs abiding ethical (societal) baseline

- Need to distance personal elite rewards with the love life of staff members and their families, or impose blatant formalities and protective withdrawal allowance schemes, possible with compensations attached

- Disbelief the elite should have any personal access to volunteers when everything costs and they specifically hold many resources as a center of their importance to begin with (elite plus mutually benefitting accords)

Sacred Sites Travel Ethics

- Ease of contradictions as promoting on premise, purified introduction in/of influence

- Areas setup to enjoy the emotionally driven, fantasy, or conceptual as states of being, possibly compartmented as to avoid interaction with each other as highly differentiated premises, such as with enjoying areas dedicated to arrangements segmented across or with

- Creative fantasy

- Intellectual scenarios

- Feel good cultural sensibilities (development of taste, feelings in relation to food, products, sensory)

- Theatre accounts

- Used as medicinal treat, in context of stress relief, will to live, and feeing cared for and   loved in virtue of having, scribing/confirming values and meaning

- Potential graduating across experiences, to form an embodiment of experience, from each specialist's performers, setups therein as on premise configurations default (traditions)

- Version just of politicians, expected required and cost more, yet not necessarily open to those with more income, such as in similar reasoning of the conformity of class arrangement based on civics forms of preoccupation (security risk levels as possible so called classes/ratings of associated measures of safety protocols)

Development of infrastructure over time

- Fundamentals to life

- Transportation

- Faith as stability feature

Cultural Feature of Scientific Networked Resources (Festivities secured)

Determining size of cultural-asset to be achieved

- Establishing how much default practice/training is required to meet minimum standards

- Limiting administrative level to size of potential pool of candidates for assignment

    - Assumes declines in ability to operate as signs of corruption

    - Assumes corruption is found by the means they use as damaging/wasteful/neglect

    - Assumes invasion trying to ruin operations will attempt to create incorrect data for   analysis

- Measuring religious membership/participation by conformity in virtue of attendance, events esteemed, and other testable, calculable, and otherwise assumed civics enabled as protected

- Establishing reference data in connection to natural and fabricated contamination of nature as edible, or drinkable, as general means of deliberation

- Designing public sport and spectacle to naturally augment or decrease in stature of accommodations, along elite standings thus per individual of fame deriving naturally more fanfare, audience, *funfair challenges as likely source of abuse

- Determining long-term gloried state of appeal, is found to be ancient and ongoing in enjoyment, may assume museum class of image building (luxurious deployment of otherwise not usable commercially, yet implemented by civics/state as heritage or cultural site supported by nationalism)

- Use of large-scale landscaping models to forge areas into grand, simplified events themed enjoyment of so called majestic

- Use of large-scale geographical, or stellar formations as part of the esthetic and designs in which the natural majesty is itself dwelled into, as careful deliberation of virtue in configurations with esteem

- Development of infrastructure to suite ritualistic application

- Securities required to intercept foreign invasion, and ability to monitor larger scale movements as suspicious and not tolerable as peacetime so called, yet without specific reason or care to explain massive scale of movement beyond admitting their entry will create dire need and their conformity is predictably nonexistent, their stance somehow protected as their own, whose movement is too massive not to be organized by level of authority akin to government, military, etc. Predictably, requires potentially stealth means of mass relocation of target arrival and disposal services signed into as waste management to their contributing effect.

- Development of naturally producing, or naturally benefitting from infrastructural material-conversion, such as to fortify walls, structures

- Overall calculations and coordination's to help local areas and incoming to bridge into connectivity the financial stability through policies adhering securities of an assumed formal mandate (written and accessible as obvious standards here abide, explained as simplified, yet layered as without leaving individuals to seek management bypass as if allocated in policy)

    - Assumes civics configuration does allow for individuality to attain management through proper licensing, as possibly educational resources etc., therein as packages subscribed into

- Assessing territorial markers and the premise if any, of regional support configurations, which are assumed required modified per larger changes in boundaries/levels of authority

- Reserved elite routes such as to ease shipping, political or authoritative movement as mentionable, as non-conflicting to patriotism, yet of stealth routes perhaps not allowing assembly to manifest, as travel and move forward only, and possibly at specific non-public hours such as for the transportation of mass value/danger goods or materials.

- Sacred sites, such as that enable the building/region to be called a sacred site, and therein a network of connectivity therefrom

- Security allocations for capital, in which the area is emptied of non-securities formed/trained peoples

Stellar-Guard Command
Scientific Networked Resources - Head Office

Communication Connections Informative Network

- Connection to all public buildings, internal status summaries

- Formal registry of festival/traditions granted-verified premise, license owners, and attached regulations

- Heritage & patriotism, record of sanction heroes

- Securement of authoritative ceremonies, capital class action-sequence, alert

- Achievements presentation, public areas, monitored discretely as likely indicator/canary source that spies, invasion, corruption will engage against

- Trophy avenues, display sectors, showcasing larger regional context such as based on energy source of technology, based on large scale living embodiments, or orders of faith such as empires of faith

Stellar Mobile Empiric Instillations

*Stability of trade through faith compliance in administrative compatibility as system performance evolved

Civics as held in sanctuary within faith as Acari-boundaries and Yawaeh ID, intellectual property and contractual obligations/source materials-registrations as safe kept across duplicate specifically as program-service instillations

Trade as secured by crypto currencies conforming to network configurations whose breach activates military defense, onto offensive empirical powers of immediate intervention

Military Campaign as securing faith, as wrath engaging, as Omni potencies possibly without end, the end is not, and not safe until termination notice

- Pastoral protections as enabling succession of so called new campaign per appointment limited to less than rural as transferred divine right to conflict as unified known in default virtue of Animal kingdom

- Assumes right of war only possibly within an ecologically sound development in protection of the represented species overall

Cities as developed in accordance to mass density expectation

Region as having to adapt customs in regulation of differing (per region) supplier, whether, and other onsite resource and associable behavior policies conforming to, as expectation general integrative with/to integrity as solidification mechanism (recognition of author as Systematic Christ to all regions abridged).

Pastoral as animal kingdom liberty in connection o origins as naturally promoting system wide, thereby potential cleanse, augmentation to natural facilities yet of an esthetic and function awareness appeal to resource-origins, long-term dietary in relation, reflections to our own placement in hat cycle of conformities as subject to both fabricated and naturally inclined conditions (onto conceptual, and science orientated assumed long term faith applications thus coherently so)

*Resource development as key asset: build, finder, per major societies of influence

Infrastructure/territorial markers set as in determination, strategic involvement in:

Routes as general stellar pathways or established ground roads

Cross ways/travel points that bridge such as through transfer of ID allocations as point of entry/transfer, requiring physical presence assumed

Waterworks/liquid-centers as connecting to vitals across systems of abundance gathering/cultivation

> Default Services as
>
> - Constructions in relation/whose supply of fabrication are using-significantly water/liquid safety for usage compliant (ecofriendly as likely in moderation total)
>
> - Repairs as having to initiate along budgetary terms of expectation, including for transformative upgrading or reformation building
>
> - Mapping/Communications – Records keeping and resource allocation securement, perpetually derived as in advance to conflicts and plights in form of secured bureaucracy, whose specialized viewpoints, policy building are inclined to ready for common statistical, predictable regional custom application/circumstance, and overall developmental trends actually considered, yet having to do (predictably) with biological, technological, or orderly s empires of faith in connection to political so called securement as pledge/principal, oaths and policy (require formal, written) yet involving reformation (easing across transformative era shifting trends as layering not likely total revolution based).

Political traditions as policy to institutions as infrastructural framework supporting literature

> - Limitations on history and culture, as reserves of appreciated, market available products, as units, models, sampling (limiting features embedded, assumed)
>
> Considerations: *Profitable, enjoyed, bypass as vital trade network?
>
> - What means to secure market place as profitable in relation to political tyrannies assigning no limitations to self, claiming to represent free markets yet apposing them using government, national or international resources

Civics cultural traditions centers as in appreciation to authors, designers, emerging innovative, inventive talents

- Limited as in concern as history for species in relation to the image of God as involving intelligence, in the influence of species using language

- Performance and assessment as per level of established achievement, thereby student as separate to learnt for competing

Heritage network, as systems encompassing the totality as remaining complete, yet as recognized movement, remain updated as would the knowledge desired of placements, implications (what protections where embedded?)

- Historical events in continuity of a timeframe for reasonable, or inspired references for development

    - Exploring state sanctioned legends

- Discovery of natural phenomenon converted into technological measure

    - Reflections on how to map, introduce, use or apply

        - Time, eras,

        - Space, geographical features per categories of organization

        - Visual arts as natural development of individual and as cultured of naturally developed/learnt appreciation of perspective

        - Explorations of species and their categorization of image/comparing actives

        - Learning system functioning defaults applicable as strategy, not necessarily by name or scientifically pronounced function, and thereby two testing scheme, one memorizing key terms as scientific, the other function to purpose based as cultural-strategic perspective

- Historical development, how where major cities of assumed touristic, cultural appeals forged, development, are they of importance on either depicting development of terms or overall strategic formations as appreciative of civic, cultural enabling

    - Noteworthy policy leadership, such granted, considered founding fathers/members having enabled policy important in relating to species overall development in which the term nation/country and its proposed culture is validated thus

    - Establishing parameters of, what, why is era common, common to what perspectives   in relation to policies, standards, and results

- Adventure programs as creating tamed approaches to wilderness explored

    - Safeguards against liter and contamination

    - Signage as protective policy and then within entry, as built on premise, such as in development of a story combining bits of detail along a path of trajectory, and a reinforcement of premise in both title or theme of location, and at exiting as farewell in appreciation of knowing

- Creating custom maps to then use as reference guides on sites, enabling team leader as navigations and inventory, such as in connection having assumed first aid, a backup communications and or including persons responsible for, as basic adventure team building requirements

Trade: Administrative Centre

- Must have fastest paced reaction in/with policy, assumed slowest, most difficult to change long term policies such as set until exhaustion, or set until project completes

Culture/Regional Image: Administrative Centre

- Regulates policies concerning respecting conformities of traditions forging, testable/observable in performance of loving virtues, and beauty personified (from what, to what premise, to what standards in comparisons of established as a series of held policy conforming membership to long term participation of select specialization within/among destiny qualified in God's empire

Wrath: Administrative Centre

- Species defense and allocations of strategic forces, policies and adaptation spheres

Jupiter Systems Administrative HQ, location or purpose of centralized function in appreciation to largest base of resources as Key/Vital systems by category of function:

- Agriculture and time/schedules/advisory notifications associable

- Hospitals & Hospitality, monitoring secured state of international interaction/domestic ability to self-satisfy, networked ability to cultivate a difference efficiently

    - Careful consideration of urban already invested into, and rural as awaiting if equal opportunity or opportunity to/for the impoverished, less fortunate then of development systems conforming to domestic development as securement for all entries such as from supplies rendered meaningful

- Language & Diction – Safeguarding meanings in attribute for formalities of overall destiny, of culture as in God's direction, as in development in elevation to traditions (faith as empires assumed integrated through ascension as systems awareness standard in expectations compute, conform

Ships: Administrative Centre

- Ground as assumed in waters

- Ground/stellar as limited to transportation, whose fuel source active are to an imminent threat to all life such as on planet

    - Stellar as with propulsion systems not subject to or not authorized to embark upon (planetary) gravitational forces

Civics/Faith abridgement: Marriage Administrative Centre

    - Limited to concentrations of, for marriage, membership plans for those married

    - Purification rituals for those would-be or married

    - Seals of initiation, certificates or awards of anniversary or otherwise contractual obligations achieved/success

Status update as required in regards to terms and associated information and a status-change/verification mechanism

- Securities training in relation to monitoring, or assassination

- Foreigner: Which country

- Staple goods: Subsidized products listing

    - Specific food allocations reserved for soldiers and the poor such as in terms of holiday

    - Celebration of a humble yet nourished perspective

- Elite standing - Bloodlines self-monitored/registered in appreciation to delimitations such as living (so called disposable) in the capital, and thereby requiring extra embedded securities features in relation to invasions

Tribute/Premise Function-Based event as cultural reserves established by powerful leaders

Relevancy in regional title, in reservations as administrative ground world/base limited to administrative and trophies

    - Not celebratory

    - Not for tourism of any non-interested/non-owners

    - No room, area, building unsearchable

- Patronage registry as, financed, supporting innovative visions nationally, regionally signed onto

- Collection of value examples, of non-movable product examples such as potential construction, power source systems, experimental testing of non-mass destruction status material/components

- Exposition as trade network hosting sites

- Secured as without contradiction permitted, regions of area as do not tress pas under any circumstance

    - Banishment from malfunctioning global positioning device as must be on the way leaving, with no guarantee of survival provided

- No temple may be dedicated to this planet/regional instillation

- Not a mass refuge site

- No reserve for music or demands on live musical performance including the potential to include musical

Festive/tournaments/ reserves relevancy in regional title, as Administrative ground world/base limited to administrative and games, celebrations

    - Requires those arriving to pledge on having common victories, of having victory/achievement/noteworthy status such as signed for by national default as leeway potential

    - Using parts of attendance income, internal production mechanisms for military and to   feed poor during holiday

    - Careful not to appreciate, use volunteers, area restricted even if purely games and celebration in motto themes expected, conductive to the species home world allocation of Jupiter standing confirmed into vigor/fortitude

    - Site limitations, no explanations on the technology and building of structures kept on planet/stellar-instillation

**Expected tasks of priority for the regional government, collection of income or tax, regardless of the motto claim of utter power or importance in the area as a victory center

- Routes, vital nourishment

- Fountains

- Landscaping, appealing themes

- Cinematic and theatrical or other performances

- Tournaments arrangements, including fixed locations of specialist activity/performance

- Racing courses

- No circuses, nor gladiator like excuses for bringing in odd, strange, non-conform participation in mass

- Garden spaces yet not enabling any institutional usage of private sector grow operations where instillation is equipped to manufacture refinement of produce such as into potential poisons, or so called medical application beyond traceable sedation, and bandages or wound dressing

- No temple may be dedicated to this planet/regional instillation

- Regional environmental and pollutions monitoring

- Display galleries, and fabrication standards for on-site, quick rebuilding operations and maintenance

    - Site potential of giving away whatever the people can grab, carry of so called state issued goods (regional), as trophies and products of a completed (paid for) events phasing to a next theme, project of development

- Not a mass refuge site

- No reserve for music or demands on live musical performance including the potential to include musicals

Performance Evaluations – From/for Across the Scientific Network of Resources

- Assigned tasks history

- Task premise vs. task as completed summery

    - Quality index, verified status of completion, state relevancy for assessing determination

- Notes summery for: Evaluation/Performance/ Results gather

- Routes, territory covered, territories included in permission or licensing

- Formal audiences expected, routes, territory covered, territories included in permission or licensing

- Highlight comments of visiting celebrity, recognized or otherwise esteemed talent/guests

    - Can be membership based, may require censorship in conformity to their medias, such as contractual obligation to avoid public outcry

    - Political highlights, such as from reserved areas to sit where comments may be quoted from, requiring recorded validation of available content grantable

- Purchasing of dedications, including as ownership, patronage claims

- Vocabulary requirement as pro victory, and does not compute self-defeating on terms of so called strategic defenses, assumes invasion attempting to bridge into formalities to break formal harmony of premise

    - Multi lingual translated for sending off media as communications station, thereby enabling public language support to be limited to planetary host

- Development of quick response translation into communications outward (voice showing up as in proper language of anticipation

- Ban on fighting animals as sport

- Honoring formal founders of celebrations & trophies platform possible as in God's direction. Limitations on historic accounts, cannot conform to reckless endangerment as enjoyed/enjoyable, and may lead to the termination of any would be usage of roman era relic

Planetary Requirements regarding celestial bodies reserved as celebration platforms/spacing

- If taxation is increased, transit to leave the planet must be given to those not willing to pay, with the transport fee, and faith/civics pledge of accepting conformity, added if they want to return

- Location is not to be a strategic location of conquest in relation to nearby vital energy based, technological, biological of faith driven systems of vital importance

- Greek & Roman strictures of theme welcome, limited to the planet, not to become nor forge empiric expansion

- May be a requested site of high political, or authoritative execution, or suicide, possibly public if by necessity?

- Must be consented to, cannot be brought under false guise

- Allowed to have a reincarnation blessing, and undertake cleaning rituals for ready, as refreshed body, technological performance, and will, spiritual strive, pledges in secret oaths to faith as in God's empire/direction assumed most celebration-worthy/trophy win.

Performance Status Info

- Lists of completions

- Context summaries as

    - What are system standard/averages per category designations?

    - Is the planetary standard far off from the systems averages?

    - Grounds for class categorization, enabling potential gambling per performance of acute performance possible (assumed possible)

        - Not acceptable as non-intelligent participation, as war only embodiments devoid of faith's ability to have forged wrath as nevertheless light hearted

        - Potential to enable blood bathing, sold as commodity

            - Signs required if do not drink, do not entertain, do not show-off

- Women's or specifically non-gendered performance may include being excluded from parts of or entire cities, if designated to fighting games, such as by species, or by virtue of species in faith specified

Luxury Bathing & Pools

- Formulated for expensive, individual, romantic, or communal as filtered pools not for bathing

Pledge Temples/Churches

- Thematic Accords to Membership/Programs & Volunteer based training assumed (contractual obligations required formal, upfront and of limited duration and or of relevant access in relation to market value having reaches proper/stated levels of abundance

Museum

- Potential city (touristic) state

    - Excludes all capitals

Touristic reserves donated for medical staples distribution

    - Planting of mass medicinal flowers while preserving landscape from tampering, yet building for touristic observation as self-financed potential

    - Use of production such as in connection to education for the development of science in relation to naturally sourced medicines samples/prototypes-development

    - Limitations on ownership as requiring royalty to civics non transferrable

- Clarification, repayment through creation of income generating companies as not the purpose completely, requires inability of supreme to use public asset and own scientific pursuits, of which government already has priority or option for emerging industries regarding facilitation/infrastructural development and formal investment plans

- Requires public stocks, such as crypto attached, of-simplicity/in-response-to that all endeavors for public good/satisfaction

- Clarification tyranny areas not excluded from requirements, unless all markets enclosed as no trade whatsoever per all industry, not pet industry (paid as contact not on tyrannical whim)

Hospitals - As networked, Emergencies Administrative Centre

- Emergency response, action-reaction to epidemic programs

    - Investigation of causes, symptoms, treatments relating to anything found to be killing people in the thousands

    - Investigation abuses regarding standards proposed as diagnoses due course, or due diligence, and operations whose results are non-conforming to public general expectations

    - Laboratories for dissecting/autopsy

    - Requiring defaults of 4 or above related yet not all financed by same interests in participating

    - Encourages traditions invested into system care across systems based on own authorship/experimental success

        - Assumes traditions formations is state sanctioned, sign of oppression of faith if having no means of status-recognition yet producing industry wide upgrading in facilitation and infrastructure

- Awards and scholarship programs such as for patronage accords limited to 25% long term

    - Limited to programs as stated, not useable for terms such as all expenditures thereafter if not mentioned such as by industry, project, market standard, or all inventions thereafter, terms of service

    - Cannot be traded for tuition amounts given away as credit, must be given as finances, which are then usable by individual

- Food reserves/food storage

    - Annual harvest festivals within refreshing surplus emergency stocks (Thanks Giving)

    - Testing of foods for contamination, sewage, exposer damages

- Treasuries

- Storage of overstock, such as to protect markets of price dumping

- Fees as potentially percentage of stock for storage, grading, and receipt/administrative services

- Clear division between dry and wet/armored/specialized goods stored

Monuments

- Privilege buildings, requires complete formality among respective membership, with potential for state to intercept non deliverance, false profiles of reward and slander, conspiracy to omit founders and premise (assumed compatible to integrity, in alignments to registered themes of faith or civics policy of obligation

Internal Securities/quality control policy

- Call to uniform per industry, vs. non-standard principals considered tyrannical or invasive

- Intervention potential on foreign attempts to use domestic uniforms

- Potential usage of faith and national symbols, including contractual and considered patronage in context of industrial cross-national obligations as contracted into services conforming to national/empiric values/interests

- Self-monitoring for conquest conspiracies, such as the creation of misleading assets, resources, and breakthroughs exposed only during night or off-hours

Refugee Sanctuaries

- Labor refugees (specific limitations to specialized industry, until re-application as thus non refugee)

- Intellectual refugees (specific limitations to specialized industry, until re-application as thus non refugee)

- Dedicated communications and habitat allocations, secured, in agreed upon seclusion potentially

Administrative & Scientific Performance evaluations

(Regarding inter-personal relations standards assessment of options/obligations summery creation)

- Examining highly-specialized scientific language only readable by advanced scientific systems of interpretation/operational-methodology

    - Looking for monopoly schemes

    - Looking for riddles of conjuncture

    - Looking for fragments intended incomplete as to enable a system elsewhere as   informally driven/ (operated under no guidance, nor abiding premise of formal invested interest)

    - Examining system organizations and comparing current to previous, and transfer into future new groups, for possible invasion/replacement-tactics

    - Artistic appeal as used over tasteful and technical formations as indicator

    - Examining destruction of sites where no or little evidence remains as default requirement, including hidden default monitoring devices

    - Coordinating carefully victory celebrations with specialist security forces

    - Analyzing censorship policies in relation to formation intent, purpose

    - Looking for so called watchful security offensively extreme, assumes a general harmony standard for influence

    - Enabling differing gendered customs, or segmenting as to impose agreed upon policy, even relationship standard while contracted, co-workers

    - Formality of request as potentially discrete, yet placed in securement of history log
non delete until end of project as possible terms of contractual responsibilities

- Assumes all parties must have live recording and may involve non usable unless specifically contract breaking related

      - Potentially requiring the insertion of reasons why relationships may proceed with delimited physical interaction

      - Potential to affirm marriage membership clauses, access, potentially excluding marriage membership clauses yet requiring formal mention to membership

      - Potential usage of membership exclusive services, such as specifically industry, career and lifestyle orientated, with a quality rating that requires group to re-vote principals

            - Assumes some members will needless seemingly mindless entertainment, relief, and others will need high end intellectualism, and that mixing the two is not actually possible as predictions of female participation as trained or performing

                  - Artistic as possibly seemingly both, such as under scripted form where a specialized program tells them what to say (if able to use person's matrix (personal information setup)

Administrative & Scientific Performance Standards for appreciation

- Clarity and concise to thesis, while also attaching expanding references of secondary notes and observations assumed formulated, such as indicated if fragment/fragmented

- Realistic, including of resource, of possibility to require complex layering of supply chain development, factoring in new sources of reference/resource

- Possibility as statistically inclined, if not realistic as having been determined or existing yet

- Able to abridge existing systems of contemplation, demonstrated natural ease/tendency in design as functional-driven, assumed thereby assumptions clarified as secondary

- Ownership stakes, clauses, claims

- Within secured timeframes, developmental cycles

Administrative & Scientific Performance Standards for quality standards

- Conform, compliant, computes

- Secured

- Assembly of persons as a group, a team with leadership and direction

- Augmentation of knowledge as formulated, and separation yet augmentation of references knowledge, with compartmented, secured

- Creating sympatric environments of harmony as encouraged, themes arranged to enjoy not (necessarily) distract

- Safeguard on those arriving with so called clearances or academic titles, for an in-house function based testing, such as with knowledge of pivotal obligations and responsibilities required for the determination/operations of work

    - A potential guard against those involving any level of honor, in that the completion of that project is the only priority of honor, of gaining honor

Administrative & Scientific Identification

- Biological origins

- Nation(s) or region(s) technological learnt

- Formal academia titles

- Relevant ethical considerations, information surveyed, kept to cultivate an orientated/trained environment

- Personal achievements, such as including hobbies, sports, personal notations

    - Including honorable mentions yet as secondary

- Status of completion among faith projects pledged to, if existing

    - Potential fabrication of predictions clauses and expectation, for those requiring   secured or defensive facilitation to proceed with works

- Personal training, fitness plan, if required monitory listed such as to activate group custom gym, sports & fitness areas

- Possibility to mention financial assets, such as to secure long term members for participation in anticipating future projects, assumed non conflicting

- Notes that highlight others must be favorable to the person whose profile is defining personal standards/expectations/imagery

- Favorite inspirational, faith and other harmony quotes, works

- Recording for formal public appearances, performances, assumed practical categories:

    - Artistic Workers (liberal arts, and or specific specialized, formal arrangement to upgrade through training/workshops offered, civics orientations)

    - Dream-Workers

    - Poetry

    - Wisdoms

    - Musical

Administration of Selections Inventory

(Major themes approved, aligned to integrity formulated into appreciation)

- Spring

- Water

- Woman's slight self-grooming, onto forms of expender in model/exemplified form

- Honors due to faith

- Fountains if enabling love

- Heights within splendors

- Tracing a tragedy to the decision at the scene of contemplation

- Dexterity of a form/form-enabling dexterity (animal, sports, design)

- Catastrophe of an incorrect vote

- Gardens

- State of art (showcasing) agricultural along its leading technologies

      - Can mean strong, model animals, fertile lands

- Transformations of a divine nature, yet limited to strategies in influencing awareness

- The heat/spotlight of performance

- Carvings relating to traditional/classic literature

- Scene of abundance with locals enjoying fruits/products/conditions of labor

- Glorified images with titles of whom, from local coinage

- Riddles in consideration of natural phenomenon (natural forces)

Stellar Network Science Premise - To adhere long-term stability in manifest of faith's objective methodology/operations/development of/for destiny

- Physics   - Chemistry   - Astronomy   - Geology

Resulting Observations Predicted

- Forces based on observable combinations of matter, whose origins equate categories of common-force energy traditions as/of development, of an eventual/findable source

> - That matter and energy is/are, can be (potentially) blended/cause-involve as-to-modify into creation of further specialized blends/results

(Resulting Observations Predicting the changing results assumed stable in virtue of a combination of matter and energy as interacting/developing tradition of previous creation/modification)

- The use of temperature, assumed as a tradition of increasing/decreasing energy, to modify conditions set

- The use of substances known to attract or repel each other to control as a tradition of energy setting-creating/retracting/compacting

> - Use of controlled movement set to differing potencies of consequence in relation to medium traveled across

- Observing overall changes of resulting form/potencies, by measurement of physical properties or the effect upon physical properties set to establish connectivity of reactionary

> - Using the end conclusion of what is found to be stable outcomes after transitions, to then predict the source as present based on results found, cataloged, kept as vital reference

> - Measuring the level of brightness or dim in results, as well as (possibly undetermined) frequency-adjusting-variables and duration (contrasting, distinguishing factors, such as used to categorize methodology and result find calculations)) within modifications

- The attempt to purify substances to produce similar or acceptable results, minimizing overall toxic potencies, or derived issues altogether as possible/probable

> - The potential securement in confinement of toxic substances to create far greater yields notable as traditions of power, or modifications to matter

- Observing the long term, far end impact of industrial usage, such as if, when detectable within the atmosphere

> - A prioritization on the importance, development of monitoring, filtering, protection of living vitals for water, air, heat in relation to toxic results per traditions of energy used, or in relation to the modification of fabrication assumed in an industrial context

- Determining the chemical property, as matters form of a tradition of energy, instead of what may be categorized as the study of forces, impact, and other consequential affirmations of trust (trusting references, yet objectively developing sensory, methodologies/intelligence)

- Determining the impact of matter and traditions of energy upon living beings, whose movement of inner systems is assumed a closed yet interactive/absorbing system, yet in relevancies to potencies such as observed by measures of distance/ or distance of measures per scientific course of overall explanation assumed each abiding an objective trajectory if/when applicable to the conformities of realities and status of what is, known space (reference building principal, adjustment principal to the continuity of our fabric as an embodiment of matter whose tradition of energy is fragile and unique among compositions that (relatively) are not

- Observations of larger examples of long-term build up, whose majestic nature is that of the very landscape considered there/their custom-regional locality

   - Temperature based/modified regions such as having only or mostly specific trends of matter, having gone through specific and similar traditions of energy such as areas

      - Ice and glaciers

      - Sand, earth, and other considered land, ground composites, in which as natural thereby the combined systems of matter and traditions of energy manifest as domestic life are assumed in harmony

         - Intervention to isolate, reduce, remove dangerous contaminations such as infringing upon those not knowing/organized/able to cleanse/utilize/avoid

Reminders regarding principal in affiliation to resulting observations

(The difficulty or impossibility of so called natural law using purely matter, traditions of energy to interpret fundamentally complex, dynamic forms of evolving onto potentially mindful configurations of layered, adaptive functioning)

- That geography if examined too closely (without altering natural movement/appearance or other sensory application of interpretive onto perceivable trends for analysis), is always in movement due to the overall traditions of energy enabled the living systems to become mindful of their environment

- That geography too far away does not reveal the in-depth modifications useful to build references

- That in the fields of matter, traditions of energy, and their combination/emergence as chemical or biological, moderation tends to favor resulting outcomes, yet moderation is/can-be also relative to extreme conditions of comparisons in itself

- Scientific papers as having to be mindful our development is a regional-custom in regards to so called natural composition or evolution of/from/towards itself, and as onto manifest destiny as perpetually driven accord of omnipotence (science-faith driven accords)

- A concern and excitement that development and change of our environments can occurred very rapidly

- That the most important of discoveries must both be made formal, and must remain hidden usually in context to the dangers of their proximity to life or especially to the potential modification/danger towards all life especially (in regards to safety measures where invasions seeking supremacy are not ours, nor in God's direction)

- The need to adjust authoritative protection, possibly, as well as self-termination protocols upon projects found to be within tyrannical accords revealed and assumed informal at initiation

- The consideration of what vital systems cannot be commercial, such as relevant to the transitioning of mass matter, or traditions of energy, chemical processing, or biochemical composition/form

- Communications equipment as a potential example needed safeguard along defaults in which literally shape/confine/enable regions to function based on specific resource driven such as technological/traditions pursuits

- Trying to remain interesting (appealing to non-conforming as specialized, differing age groups) or fascinating (clear concise to field, expertise)

- Reinforcement of science as traditions conditioned/promoted among juvenile (undetermined in which overall pursuits in lifestyle, career, or pledging willing to undertake)

- Personal/default satisfactory as being able to understand or explain the performance being undertaken/conducted

- Creating of/by means to evaluate memorization of all (relevant) details as understanding components of performance

- Creating of/by means to explain the strategic involvement of performance, such as offering guidance of development, involvement as participating/member, as interacting across differing scenario of known typical yet highly specialized fields of secured accommodations/operations/methodology and traditions training/formation building

- Creation of/by artistic models/examples to influence and inspire yet arriving when performances are established and complete, being the equivalent of reporters not contributors of the science, yet potential enablers of the social conditions and wellbeing in terms of harmony and promotion of results/membership/performance

- Inquiries as having a wonderful selection, possibly, of which the study of mind in relevance to a configured sensory is further proposed as or differentiation of matter, traditions of energy, chemical, biochemical, compositions thus enabling as living propelled the sense and associated mainframe to dwell upon them

Experimentations Reminders

- That the microscopic environments have to be setup similar to the larger scale relative samples to introduce similar (if possible) contextual altering fragments of detail/effect, assumed sought after

- That the crystal form is that of a completing system whose durability/resilience as traditions with adaptive/systems reactive embedded, is/are therein model in comparisons to the composite within its developmental stage to that actuality, and therein, can be used to generate completed systems therein, static accords driven (assumed relative and possible)

Scientific Rituals & Thematic Indoctrination

(Patronage, traditions, civics-faith forging)

- The rise of smoke and revelation from darkens to consequence/brilliance action-in-action, consequential prompt

- Depicting light sources a alive, creative, as representing differing conditions

- Miracles of nature as transformative, within context curious, and the development predictably fragmented into cohesion/binding systematic

- Power as in/of rays of light

- Attraction becomes considerations of categorization

- The perfection of transparency, within analysis/methodologies applies back the speakers, assumed harmoniously

- Arrangement of small forms into displays of force, proportion/control/arrangement

- Experiments where we see the hidden details as artistically proposed, assumed not then known within one display/obvious observation

- Exemplifying massive alterations/changes, such as within landscaping features

- The contemplation of similar, as within differing states of matter, context of living/forging within space, ground, liquids, and potencies as plasma/forces in combinations of virtue (fabricated splendors)

- Chemical attraction, beyond the scope of science, sort of!

- Brilliance you shall/must see!

Associating Physical Forces to assumed cause(s) and effect(s)

- All contextual variables surrounding a chemical force

- Which trend of observations require specialized equipment

- Which trends of observation require advanced analysis expertise?

- What is required known within the measurement of each compounds in relation to their placement, volume in relation to one another?

- What does affecting contents across differing fields of energy do, if such stabilizes form or composition in itself, what does the addition entry of composition or energy further do?

- Are there common exceptions to standard conditions, can they be grouped together for consideration of an unknown relation

- What obligations are there attached to conducting specific observations, use of materials, and use of resources/configurations to enable energy?

- Can the refinement process be altered in connection to adding specific substances known to have a conductive effect in relation to the conclusion/results expected, being aims for or towards?

- What equipment must be delivered to filter away as preventing exposer to resulting substances, whose accumulated effects as refined is assumed toxic in virtue of collective absorption

- Use of materials to coat a material and increase, decrease, stabilize reactions/mode-of transfer

- Detection devices within both the transfer devices and the reaction/concluding chambers of output/exhaust, if applicable

- The transfer of matter to matter, energy to energy, chemical to chemical, biochemical to biochemical, and if they involve cycles of production/natural-occurrence, a recreation model as template of nature formed

  - Transitions across states of matter having means to diversity fields of outcome

- Creating effective formation, such as to allow natural forming movement to be used efficiently or to configure as to implement scientific (premise-function) device

- A study on the depleted form of matter whose energy therein has been exhausted, such as to enable references into finding matters of origins or abundance, or factor in likely developmental scenario and applicable strategies or guidance over determinations there involved/consultable

> - Value and circumstance deriving prioritization, such as establishing market needs, and anticipation of results as an inclination to develop/guide-support reason

> - A careful re-evaluation of absolute and or stability features, per significant discovery of scientific innovation within entire categories of industrialized progress

> - A study on material able to become the same end product/composition, such as biochemical, assumed

Illumination - Interval points along constant supply chains (such as across renewable energy)

- The ability to display smaller, into larger, more detailed aspects in appearance, distinguishing contrasts

- The variation of display to exemplify traditions of energy as spectrums of energy manifesting assumed tendencies of perspective, in contemplation of the living systems requirements per division of power structure conform

- A reminder of the overall distribution of energy as heat assumes a proximity tampering in proximity to the application of the energy itself, such as to in long term create residue of a condensed, accumulative nature

> - The monitoring of discharges into nature where long-term venting/circulation or retention in calibrated distributions thus with specific concentration areas is expected to create and accumulative result

> - Creation of filters for individual life forms or larger scale environmental features where large amount of natural resources flow, travel across a defined/finite spacing which the filter can be within within/upon

Determining (production/operations/storage-allocation capacity)

- Capping terms of reproduction in relation to overall structural context, such as to what degree of abundance can be validated within formalities of consequence

- Undue friction among the masses having chosen to over reproduce/produce as indicator of invasive activity

> - Cluttering space so no one can do any work/worth, especially for a result that was never formally approved nor sought for as indicator of corrupt/corrupting organization

- Undue size of machines where no practical advantage can be indication of attempts to downgrade areas planned by others, or a custom planning to acquire and create hidden replacement schemes

Determining a moderate usage and long term application

- The anticipated usage of machines to function along moderate usage for efficient, longer-termed duration than over usage

    - Potential after hours monitoring for sensitive or rare equipment, such as contractually obligated

- Development of knowledge as intelligence force whose momentum is safeguarded in considerations of faith including scientific endeavor, of which this text as doctrine exemplifies

- Embedding requirements of respect within communications within co-working circumstances

- Civilization as layered first, last defenses onto the safeguarding of quality determination, vital objectively towards biology, technology, systematic faith as configurations with destiny in achievements arranging/forcing harmony onto omnipotence

- Refraining from allowing the general corruption-traditions of trying to reverse or oppose as a premise of strategic formation, predictably trying to suggest mathematical memorization is in validation of their less than equal sum 0, where subset delivery is predictably none!

- Consideration, (timed, scheduled regardless of devices embedded) alerts on processes known to cause buildup of pleasure

- Expectations that things caught in motion will breach onto experimental unknown (failure of accord expected, in consequence don't built up, liberate cohesion)

- Gradual freezing as potential condensing speed matters, such as to set perpetual heat/venting points

    - Potential security shutdown per securing devices retracting service or monitored status of functioning

- Development of prolonged recording devices to capture longer, in depth spectrum perspectives requiring potentially to adapt to the timeframe portions per field of energy, assumed having impact on the inner formation's ability to exist or otherwise the rate that exposer has as effecting impact upon that deemed live, per perspective of initiated thoughts instigated into acute awareness, whose results are compelling enough to unite and traverse fields of perspective (in harmony becoming, transformative as in nature dwelled per thus category of relative field in/of action, assumed spectrum orientated

    - Relevancy to time stabilized in virtue of context of stable features found localized if/assumed in stellar

     - Assumes we exist in proportion to fields of energy promoting specific effects upon configurations causing our awareness acute/aware/responsive

    - Omnipotence as the potential enjoyment of/onto understanding all, is it applicable, more so if we are transformed, thus transformative knowledge awaits!

Equating Universal

- Faiths solidify convention into race, and if procreation is rendered membership standardized, it is a species destiny/arrangement

> - One of the first tell signs in the separation of races and species, being diet and differing biochemical reactions and thereby guidance in reservation of regional; custom application in relation to traditions, technologies application/applied

- The highly specialized nature of science and faith, conform into arrangements bound and binding, therein does this text solidify a doctrine to bind principals across empires/species of faith, onto/into God's direction!

- Payment per performance is a solid means of records indication, providing information on territorial usage in relation to securing attendance and aiding with determination on the performance as having embedded duties, such as enabled through market share/frequency

> - Potential setup of tokens, of showcase currencies

> - Displays of symbolic payment or in symbols rendered at a cultural event from romance representing limited requests to advance/mutually-approve, to use for limited amounts to consume, or as send-off, such as for funeral arrangements, assumed approved by house designated services/tributes

> - Use of specialized currency to determine board, committee and other distribution of symbolic interest/prioritization

Universal standard, qualifier for equating Universal:

*Assumes symbolic currency can be tracked, traced, provide proof of validity/authenticity, subject to protections of authority yet possibly kept in territorial frameworks of thereby custom-arrangements in domestic handling of events management (assumes complex, empowering, simplified and accessible licensing assessment)

*Assumes a treasury position important, assumes an immediate count (also such-as-digital, immediate) is conducted (based on weight, sensors, mechanical counter, size separation, color, or simply manual counts

General considerations equating validity of regional status queue

Overall considerations of individual intelligence and setups of convention in relation to their associated formality in durable functions:

- Purpose of supply and purpose

- Designs in relation to the need to have configured machines or otherwise refined skillsets of labor

- Calculation of polite vs. being annoying (annoying as action and or inaction)

    - Crying aloud about desires to spend for the sake of depleting all as grounds for fit/tantrum

- Are the advices of locals to seek further advices from the enemy?

    - As in, are they suggesting hostility to another group and encouraging you seek them?

    - Love thy enemy as meaning not to lose one's overall perspective into that of the enemy, on terms you are initially confronting them

        - As meaning, if you exemplify the enemy in a reasoned manner, you will not necessarily suffer from their assumed brutish mannerism

        - As meaning, if you remember not to exemplify the enemy, you thereby bind to the loving nature that they are known as enemy and the hidden mist of corruption are not necessarily findable

        - As meaning, to embrace considerations the enemy strategy, you can predict securement features and adapt diligently without adapting/adopting what makes them an enemy

        - As meaning, if another keeps promoting love they enemy, they cannot resent   you and must be a lamb with you?

        - Beware heaven is said to have been grown like a mind, what you wish and strive and in complete, thus the soul is found in salvations, and nothing more thus are the saving grace of the lost, until intervention/intervention is done, complete!

        - As meaning, the adaptation to another biology, technology, and faith can be due to proximity, whose contamination as intelligent design must be convinced you are a better hope and esteem to love then your enemy was to not.

        *As meaning if you had exemplified your enemy as guidance, such as based on their so-called good works, then would they be safe? Would love their strategies itself exemplify the enemy as a defeatist movement?

- As meaning if you act as a servant to those conspiring to play, pose or act as enemy, if you are a model performance whom adjusts their behavior per criteria the so called enemy establishes as sanity, will they caste you away?

  - Assumes a formality of obligations, such as contractual arrangement included. Did they breach the contract, dis you create an escape clause?

  - Is there waste control before there is request/demand for aid or ongoing support?

Examining Diligence

- Are there administrative guidelines for suspecting as cause of concern, or of having identified a disruptive tradition/traits and policy?

  - Are there traditions that associate feeling alive with hurting other people?

- Are their standards where traditions/industry is able to formally purpose government support/focus, such as conforming to political motto and possibly required announced at designated media/news conference?

- Is some only willing to be happy within embracing the misery of others?

  - Is their occupation relevant to rehabilitation or investigation, the latter requiring no indulgence of misery made public

- Are mass amount of people arriving to accuse a person, does the state have any anti invasion policy/standard of reception?

Anticipated/Worthwhile Perhaps Collections

- National

- Regional

- Royal

Anticipated/Worthwhile Assumed Collections Subject Matter

- Trade development

- Settler/colonial efforts

- Glorified affections standard to popular convention of romance, chaste, enjoyment of relationships in a diversity of expressions conforming to integrity

- Pilgrimages and relevant tombs/items (sealed, encased) if applicable

- Strategic stories enabling victories, especially peaceful overall, and conduct to God's empire in formation/expansion/stabilization

- Exploring the Art of (cultural aspects contemporary (taken for granted, long term historic and era relics) or long term esteemed upon initiation)

- Elite versions of daily lives in comparisons so standard non-specialized, non-custom application

- Then leading examples of technology, such as with introductory advertisement

- Appealing winds, sunshine, exploration & discoveries

- Valid courage

- Indulging God

- Harvests

- Then domestic Medias, including then population international samples

- Proud to join samples

- A breathless moment in tributes of victory/accomplishment

- Fortunes being told. Prizes, classes required to achieve vindication

- Achievements soulful, of soul, as complete, in virtue of completing

- Intelligent state and its development/augmentation

- Grateful souls

- Great contributions to comforts, security, overall liberties invitation/development/specialization booms

- Era forging cultural aspects

Collections Censored Materials

- Morbid, degrading as counter interesting/valued esteem from interaction with depictions of earlier interpretation or forms of accepted or established works

> - Exception as a collection of strange or exceptions thereby not glorying content or name as so called premise

- Details of how to, why, defending treason

- Night councils, such as conspiracy stories

Catacombs - Principal designs

- Use of religious for, as symbolic art

> - Symbols reserved for catacombs

> - Paintings in relations to objects found, such as of historical resemblance on purpose thus symbolically of proposed meanings, exemplified in reading, attached prayer, attached life accomplishment in premise, assumed reasonable to do so

> - Celebrity comments left for specific ritual

> - Interior corridors build to exemplify the path between life and the depictions funeral intended to signify transitioning, assumed

> - Creating the transitioning as meaningful to the person witnessing, such as to exemplify modeled performance of deceased as guide/interpretation, such as setup and labeled as approved/motto-approved by formal representation/practitioners of faith/wrath, ritual and worship

> - General gloom, with potential of a cleaning light, outer beautiful travel as leaving, exit, to exist onto light

> - Mentions of association to faith and or charities, exclamations of request there attached, recommendation, suggestions general requests made as in tribute to the premise that person agreed for, towards (assumed acceptable nature)

Prescribed Media-Supporting symbolism - In connection to the Supreme Network of Conviction/convention retention/deliberations

- Military/Securities as Battle ground as having religious symbols involved as an ethereal intervention

- Education as Science meets the origins of foundations and limitations on criticisms as include the rough sketches of science before it developed in resemblance of the poor standings of ancient or oldest possible precedence as origins, though assumed imaginative

- Military/Securities as Use of mysterious figures to demonstrate larger scale stealth allied support of the day/engagement

- General-usage as a transparency on the goal, lead in which there are substantial grief/martyrs mentioned

- Industry as Massive transport industry movements

- Education as thought provoking illustration in considerations or noteworthy fields of academic exploration, specialized interest/academic disciplines formal

- General-usage as divulging secret meanings, such as thereafter victory reached/assured

- General-usage as reverence to stellar

- Justice as the law, a lover of convention (assumes in regards of integrity integrated into system common knowledge/awareness secured)

Experimental Section as potentially Sacred Rituals/Rituals with purpose

- Vital information per select ritual of participation

- Testimonials per custom-events of engagements (action-sequence orientated)

- Formation of the well pleasing wife

- Formation of virtuous sexual encounter

    - Virtue as arrangement for relationship

    - Virtue as conformities, contractual arrangements for marriage

    - Virtue as experimentally driven (premise, scenario building, undertaking, analysist)

      - Suggested pact, non-may hold experiment against them

      - Advised policy, careful deliberations of consent, such as before (too) intoxicated if applicable

      - Avoidance of spiritual of faith guidance, and potential use of academic, or specialist material, information, thoughtfulness

- Avoidance of subject matter exterior to scenario of context being forged as experimental grounds of/for play

- Avoidance of casual, or flings, yet potential blockade on future encounter/experimentation as part of scenario building

- Privacy and invasive counter-expectations as intervention to eliminate disruptive
characters of abuse and neglect (banning people from interference, commentary, criticism, or investigating accusers for similar conduct in on formality of premise or   scenario building as terms of invasion, trouble/mischief makers

- Formalities of defining love/consent/civilized as endurance to comply with integrity, thereby common knowledge expects a level of general appreciation to health, dignity etc.

- An avoidance of linking, using patriotic (asses stable precedence meant conformed to) as grounds, means within performing experimentation

Scientific Research/Clinical-standards of operation/Documentation

(As Wholesome Approach each interrelating such as per racial, per species, or per category of specialized interest on/of as among configurations)

Racial/Species Determination/Recognition Platform

- Representative Diagrams/Maps - Bodily-Functions System Models

- Medicinal such as per organs of category (racial as segmented, species as overall inventory assumed compatible

- Compatibility matrix (personal history and statistical analysis)

- Medical statistical probabilities of success per classification/categories of division for race/species

- Surgery

- Bloodline tendencies

- Dietary histories, customs and regional standards of evaluation, treatment if attached

- Personalized regional-custom physicians (specialist in relation to segments of population such as based on race/species of introduction

- Medicines specialized with the racial tendencies of organ reaction/cause & effect/efficiently of usage

- DNA/Community Referencing

    - Hospital inventory referencing options, if applicable, see permissions/membership table

    - Autopsies analysis summaries

    - Disease control information

Scientific Research/Clinical-standards of operation/Documentation

Animals

- Exploring bodily motion

- Strength of vital organ responsible for motion

    - Further potential inspection of organs ability to perform, vs. damages to functioning or clogging to impair flow (blood, air, secretion)

    - Testing pulse and other data from inspection-techniques/devices, if applicable

    - Testing blood, air breathed out, excretion

- Inspecting default systems function ability

    - Testing senses, nervous system reactionary, and memory

- Examining for diligence animal/caretaker-guardian-trainer

- Calculating dietary needs

- Teeth, mouth, and gum, health inspection

- Examining surface of body

- Corpse autopsies

- Disease control information

General Analysis - Automated Support & Diagnoses Standards

- Primary Symptoms as disruptive to vitals required for life sustainment

- Secondary symptoms as disruptive to overall, overall changes degrading functionality

Influences in the mode of lifestyle in relevance to symptoms

- Reference materials of interest, of use in relation to strategic planning./awareness of lifestyle, medical coordination of cause and effect of healing standards reinforcing overall guidance being offered

- Notes as predictions or recommendations to relieve, remedy, fortify

- Samples of virus, tissue, or ailment if applicable, such as to be cataloged, recorded, inventoried to confirm progression of medicinal treatment or regression of sickness

- Specialized results, if new, to be sent to client/practitioner to update, upgrade medical - treatment or deliver options renewal

- Feedback on general impressions if applicable

Maturation related illnesses - Automated Support & Diagnoses Standards

- Sudden eruption of symptoms, and a reference library to try and identity the eruption there, on site based on visual and details interpretation

     - Flash warning of immediate (severity as dangerous) required steps if cotangent requires isolation, specialized treatment

- Carefully age cycles per standard symptoms, yet possible overall examination thereafter if no conclusion in typical age group found

- Assumes information of family or bloodline relevant for diagnoses, while remaining confidential as assumed membership privilege/national privilege/custom regional arrangement standard obligations for maintaining public health

- Notification/investigation of town/city spaces where the eruption found is a severe, or highly contagious sickness found/confirmed

- A reference guide of uncommon occurrences, as last exhausted resource, that each highly unique case is added into

- Dietary regiments questions and model templates

- Pregnancy complications specialist

     - Specialist midwives, such as for predictably unstable births ahead

Autopsies - Automated Support & Diagnoses Standards

- Orientated on the delicate of pleasant paperwork (that family, friends, history will be able to read)

- Sanitation suitable to the standards of illness found in local environments

- General cotangent-like containment of bodies for those having died of/in sickness

- Records station for autopsies system wide, after date of release, such as after a year of mourning passed

    - Assumes ID required to login, and ID recorded for any information accessed, with visual/secondary conformation of ID is applicable

    - Possibly requiring anonymous names, found through categorization of symptoms, analysis, classification of sickness

- General requirement of three cases to confirm diagnosis/conclusions needing to be forwarded upwards towards administration

    - Emergency status sickness as potential to send immediate investigation to find more cases

- Examining for signs of surgery, tampering, cosmetic suppliers or fabric

    - If found verification of personal history

- Analysis of bio-chemical properties of complex, expensive/highly specialized/rare operations

    - Testing of inner contents found in relation to fermentation (chemical/bio-chemical)

    - Testing fermentation for alcohol and drugs related status along absorption track/organs/applicable system vitals & alterations to fermentation process to identify presence of or long-term users

    - *Testing for known quick evaporate/dissolve for bodies deemed cannot be autopsied

    - Testing for nutritional values, sugar levels,

    - Microscope samples cross-referencing tool

    - Simplified with specialist attachment of found cross referencing indexes, of found common offenses

- Holding an inventory of decayed samples of other life form for scenario building, including aquatic life, foliage, etc.

- Fossils, skeletal, fragments as specialist/specific-scenario mode of entry of analysis (assumed 3d model building, and possible reconstruction as image for sake of general appearance standards

Administrative Strategies of Durable Traditions Forging as Premise

- Science resources networked indoctrinated as binding principal supportive, filter with/to, allocations summery adjustment, networking, launch as mobile empiric headquarters of designated large collective resources, initiative, operational performance approvers filled into formality as network access deemed privilege of state assigned, no of accomplishments and proven investment therefore.

*And with respect to author, cultural reserves, such as for the amelioration of/onto God's direction always, pending realization of already pledged as not of mixed principal virtue, regardless of a future Christ as first status exemplifying love as ultimate goal, worth and measure

- The salvation of nations is that of rendering proof as valid, uplifting testimonial, through all sectors, as into of formality, of order as in consequence we are/adhere in God's direction always (whose initiation therein validates those having had to instigate, fend, operate as successive layers of civilization, amen), for the salvation of the country is approved by judgment

- That if you approach Jupiter in a planet/solar platform dedicated to its meaning, you will have prudence and are expected to act in compliance to your stated politics if/as conforming to integrity values, and across empiric multinational accords for boarding, usage, and other operational and management expertise (evaluations, services, renderings, complete as soulful enterprises)

- Jupiter core as networking quality of lifestyle as a matrix of individuality safe kept in the premise of larger scale acquisitions of resources in gathering of all systems united in compliance, compute, forming orderly thus.

Universal Virtues across Science resources networked as bound for/as:

- Founded upon integrity as filter to express refinement of honest as earnest

- Industrious by design of initiation

- A manifestation of faith proclaimed a living bound to all emperies of faith united in layer(s) among/within God's direction or named also God's empire

- Variations in fortunes naturally create variations in strategic placement and configuration upon initiation, yet also exemplified by performance and need to prioritize into system comprehension of success driven activation

    - Augmentation/regression of space/operational-access, performance standard per level of access conducting into, yet assumed all access assessable if in/of empiric nature of multi empire, national arrangement

- Ample supply of all known antidotes not themselves too potent for typical applicability/standard-usage

- In formalities, no distinction between public and private, simply more leeway awarded for full monitoring if applicable

- If shun by an arising political structure, movement may mobilize outward to areas that were approved (proper to that formation), as to avoid further conflict, and begin full deranged extraction of a secured fashion (mostly not wasting as standard to be kept, of which the call to action of emerging political enemy configuration as grounds for leeway to create immediate offence/defense fields of blockade, fortification as withdrawing and future supply lines encompassing)

- Fancy gardens, even if non biological yet possibly organic in esthetic appearance such as synthetic recreation

- Quick capture, rapid/response-ready, movement forces as on base

- An allowance for shocking spectacles of a strategic alliance engagement in intentions, such as of formidable technological supremacy in weapons fabrication/production and inventory control/management

- As formality, a formal premise building Jupiter has, is with integrity and their relations with native local areas is a priority to act/engage as benefactor, meaning conform also to initial declarations of tribute, service, mutual destiny forged on basis of mutual compatible-compliance factors, deeming interventions of judgment thus in securement of salvation as perpetually forward, an in expansion amen.

- Allows individualized, experimental martyrdom projects (off board, ye ton board monitoring, securement of data, such as to venture into unknown for personal gain in attachment to scientific, colonial asset building (features in conjunction with availability, requires state buy out, or buy in as contractual clause of origins in benefactor adaptable as in God's direction always)

- Potential requirements to wear symbols of adherence validating loyalty confirmation

- Relationship for highly specialized fields of authority, expert rendering, use of high-level securities, facilities as standards anticipated strict, (in regards to, yet can be baited to members joining as bluntly do or die/leave) if leeway upon membership status attained understood itself, as conform to assigned obligations agreed upon, as disregarding desires to render formal is grounds for potential termination, literarily on terms that they simply need to log in, adjust option or setting, or otherwise input records with potential to create specific separation, self-removal parameters of a peaceful nature

    - A means to safeguarding form invasion in which enemy cannot, does not know the standards of living systems will allow to pass, live, benefit with

- Self-destruct mechanism a fast travel configuration such as to purposely damage specific competent, inner travel areas relevant to invasive boarding

    - Quick repair and multi optional self-destruct, rename, self as so-called oblivion emergency protocols possible. Premise as if non changeable, as relocation potentially extreme, onto transformative adaption cycles assumed requiring localized build of of standard, compliant then, there domestic features onto/towards connectivity with purpose/with-premise

- Preapproval of marriage at commencement of relationships as expected standard to initiate romance

- Being able to cite won determinations of consequence as contractual leeway, such s on requirement of total records keeping, such as to emulate later in a game, action sequence replay, and other live in, virtual, or otherwise depictions of events as accurately as possible, with assumed standards of benefit, and ability to cut our grossness

    - Gross as assumed defined by excretion, sorrow, and other terms of plan or endearment lost or rendered hopeless in the pursuit of trivial

- Potential requirements to abide be formulated in media depiction along original in secured access only, to validate assigned personality/lifestyle adherence of cross cultural participation

    - Semi live as with time delay where any block of content is noted in records

- Ointment/transitioning rituals such as to safeguard incoming membership to special projects area, adjust to environmental standards, or enable usage of security or equipment usage by proximity of biochemical activation

- Expressing any last minuet doubt before entering, and possibly awaiting delay as to further detail yet no disregard contractual obligations within a rewrite which may cause a need for an additional travel expenses, systems contribution relevancy confirmation, processing fee if applicable

- Expected Trojan/invasion tactics, replacement of ID by those being financed/financing

- Potential public duty expectations for new members, contribution fees in labor such as to proof, validate portfolio ID

- Additional payments/investments/formality-of-allocations as required for additional expeditions/ventures/summaries

    - Suggests results, achievements required in completed fashion

Performance Standard for Academia

- Teacher may not give personal bias against state sanction lectures on heroes

    - Heroes not to be shown as juveniles, unless state no longer accepts what its origins are as formality also mentioned

        - Academic institution may be broadcasted over media and denounced without delay

        - Law abiding premise set as unacceptable must explain fortitude of common bond associated with circumstance in question, or being considered an issue

            - Must include all parties there empowered of national recognitions

- General prospect as adhering in compliance to recommendations, trajectory of teacher, including if teacher enables leeway non-conform standards to expectations of academic significance expected assigned merit/reasonable marking

- General guidance to public as gentle

    - Depicting perhaps traumatic historic accounts in relation of their frustrations of the day if approved by formalities such as written, media-refined, etc. (example state self-appointed/accepted dramatic accounts of administrative living/performance)

- Not to include combat gymnastic, yet potential relevant default extensive strength and mobility training

- Exemplifying, performing, attending summer, autumn festivities

- Careful consideration of ecological, social impacts in relation to business forums and company culture designing custom-regional holiday application

- Exemplifying marriage as special events, of interest, spectacles of respectability (as designed, as anticipated code of conduct/performance/adherence

- Learning differing eras of common life, such as across classes of living, including responsibilities associated to differing forms of leeway, assumed approachable content

- A reflective exemplifying of collage and universe lifestyle, policies, general standards of success

Educations Disqualifiers

- Intellectual limitations as too creative only

- Too efficient/memorized to have creative leeway

- Enjoyment of all too primitive conducts, which are nevertheless rehearsed, trained, or an invasive or piracy class of annoyance

On Site Empiric Role - Sanctioned as

- Emergency reformation of administrative control/policy center(s)

- Implementing class easement in regards to avoiding inter class association if counter to contractual arrangement, such as if a cheating affair in addition to a non-compatible one, in addition to a clearly breach of securities

> - Easement such as to compartmented work groups across regions where the class distinction of a public informative gather is rendered equalized by performance or orientation towards specifically compatible administrative which differ in class due to audience of participation rather than class distinction in regards to custom, policies conforming, and counter intuitive decoding of strategies as part of situational awareness, whose system configure to device/devise

- Assigned by state authority voted in under motto to perfect a specific location, thereby limited duration to political placement, with the potential to remain based on performance to contractual standards initiated as/towards

- Forming a merchant connection, or of managing larger tribute into deigning/construction/development as facilitation, in dedication towards specific elite aspect, premise approved of formal (public ceremony initiation standard as likely required, assumed important)

> - Potential industrious allowances/dedicated funs to form a supportive trades/university discipline in application of, such as technological/biological, other systematic pursuits of completed (system building/feature-programming)

- Investigation to why the area is being abandoned to foreign occupation, or invasion-like forces

- To implement system wide encouragement towards fruitfulness/abundance in worthwhile results

> - Rather a principal than contractual obligation, yet requiring filling out examples perhaps

- Creating specialty access programs for mothers, such as to encourage their knowledge to be both concise as pro specialist, and nurturing as overall generation/traditions as promoting regional custom tendencies (perhaps so) of trust, acceptance, welcome communications

- Maintaining elite access and consideration of relevancy of standings as protected by virtue of limited entry, required fees, required ownership and or granting limited access to those somehow being politically demanded to participate

> - Do not disgrace clauses as added standard

- Re-examining regional tax collection and regional support allowances, including long term heritage and other reserves intended to suit nationalist, domestic material gain

- Edifying literacy programs so include hierarchies of business formations, such as by providing a range of literature and a categorization table per division of specialist referencing (deemed vital per corresponding industry of interest, assumed standing)

- A careful examination of specialist introduction to raise value of individuals through orientations, where specialist can return to typical administrative works thereafter

> - Assumes having more of less education does not equate more thought or thoughtfulness than adding layered perspectives of specialist therein, yet with evaluation standards or needs and concerns can be addressed for the fortification of individual's contemplation-worth

> - Assumes the mind as a specialized has a finite arrangement or wills to categorize, process, perform as natural vigor and fortified by coworkers/co-students, family/associates, and friends/membership

- Working on the general environment of the area, such as to render facilitate up to international standard of high-performance education

- The instillation of new academic disciplines, as a potential re-examining of so called vital as become non conform to technological, biological, of systematic application in rendering

- Potential correction of founding principles of location, such as due to a collapse, bust, or otherwise completed premise elsewhere, or simply not as anticipated and therein having possibly adapted incorrectly over time, in anticipation of an incorrect formula/formulation

> - Testing consistencies of proposed breakthrough, such as on probationary terms, and creating resource allocations for the updating of facilities required to add new layers of technologically reinforcing, biologically reinforcing, or faith as systems complete

- Education having to tradition in relation to using highly technological personals in activation, sequence, regards

Cultural Caution Points of/for Reference Building

- If the state can no longer project, create national prestige along historic figures, having to perhaps create fictitious marvels only, such s to try and subjected then tyrannically assumed, is there an issue within the overall devising of the democracy no longer able to exemplify a model as publically acceptable, interesting, thus a tale sign of a failing empiric cultural support

Marriage within a Scientific Network of Resources assumed Secured

- Marriage as encouraged within similar standings of specialized or academic performance building

- Marriage that do not meet up to membership or entrance criteria, have the potential to reach stature, be realistic and have faith (good luck, consider what efforts are required)

- A potential options building from differing approved cultural societies, such as in support of regional custom convention, with requirements attached required

    - General opinion, warning, concerning, blessings attachable as cultural context, possible with required lifecycle comprehension in form of specific media, training, orientations, experiences, adventure training, perspective building and overall disciple and specialist activity generator (assumed obvious breeding program relevancy, or heritage support civics formations)

- Careful listing of specific marriage approved with specific divisions and possibly reinforcing/abridging creative-implementations interactions expected, such as to remind parents the child will be able to choose those details for themselves, cannot include partial recognition of themes of faith yet acquire full membership, support, coverage in access, privilege without significant resource/wealth, projects results as contributing in formality of design (assumed applicable, approvable, possibly needed extra permissions)

- Careful permissions to be absent for, or required present for

- If marriage is between those with titles, formalities of expectations, duties, and thereby conditions or obligations in relevancy to the likely administration of privileges and access

- An up to date map of differing allied posed structures and the overall powers of state over its citizenry/membership

    - Highlighted/colored display of changes, especially if kept informal

    - Monitoring as both in allied domestic as stealthy, and an open receiving monitoring as receiving

- Specific accords required formal on the so-called abandoning of a citizenship or membership, yet possibly with features and options in relevancy to shifting core of fabrication/origins

- A detailing of rights expected for the children, including privilege, resources, titles/patronage/membership if any are applicable

- Classification of service in relation to access and privileges, such as those welcome, banned, or otherwise mentioned

 - If compromises were reached, what liberty features, options were gained, what was forfeited?

 - Cultural self-void, accepts notice, as does the stated as so called non-legitimate equate nevertheless to the licensed portion have more empowerment within, over inner-personal design/configuration than faith as setup so called priority one?

Natural Ascension Principal – Forging Relics, with, for or become?

Overall, this text is for systems binding along several networks of connectivity, in proportion to designated resources vital to the future boom expansion of biology, technology, and ideally the orderly coordination of default faith to political abridgement maintaining therein of, as in God's direction and overall a resource protection accords bound, binding future destinies of, as God's empire foretold by, as Jupiter systems, network status possible, possibly arranged per galaxy, or smaller/larger specified areas of space in accordance to ability to travel, or in relevancy to time allocations of formable interest. To thus develop, expand, secure on premise accords conforming in appeal of established/establishing doctrines rendered relics worthwhile in the exploration of more.

Formula/Formulation

In reflection to ideal as judgement core, the attachment of a traditions as main attaching segment, is the proposed enhancement as such:

Quality as Durability: Ideal

Quality as per functionality in centralized: Ideal, and component support: Traditions

As Ideal: Functional Tradition – As Support: Traditions Functional

(Inner complimentary inversion)

Such as: Doing/Being

                Practice/Guidance   *As intelligence administration/formation: Guidance as doing

                                     *Therefore as complete/core: Guidance as being

Doing	Being	Being/Doing
Social Clubs	Inclusion and civics detachment	
Conceptual configurations	Traditions building and overall configurations selection	
Universality	Doing and Being	and being/doing
Conformity and scale	Compatibility mechanized and scale relevancy	
Hierarchy and glorification	Function based class and admiration/cultivation	
Individuality and destiny	Practice and guidance	and guidance/practice
Destiny and Divinity	Direction and status	
Updating, merger	Popular and adaptive	
Abstraction and reason	Formulation and purpose	
Duality and mutual-reinforcement	Considerate and expanding interested	
Gender	Masculine, Feminine, Objective	

Core of function / Function as Core:

- Survival
- Specialist
- Operational
    - Maintenance/Repair
    - Upgrade/Self-determination: Objective summery

Core of Principal

(Refinement, filters quality self-assessment)

- Archives of doubts
- Original elaborations in relation to traditions as function based reference building
- Proving, building/operating custom template
    - Determination/limitations
        - Resource anticipation, exploration, analysis
            - Expansion per overall consideration of objective/determination network

Prime as central, whose supportive tradition is set as default to ideal as control

Thereof, detachment and self-reliance of traditions as by default, securing prime/control.

Does traditions divide prime, or rather that prime as functioning is in relevance to system status, reaffirming system integrity as paramount/national-bypass configurations: Core 0.

Traditions as Group Forming

- Display lab/work-station per group function
- Display lab/work-station per individual
    - Groups Assigned
    - Groups developing as challenging
    - Groups working live
    - Groups working per industry

Healthy (based on functionality) equates into

Health...............................Ecology/Environment

Beautiful (Safeguarding the deciphering of sensual stimuli)

Beautiful............................Figure/Form

Loving (Aligning emotion reaction with idealistic instigation)

Loving...............................Sensibility

Dignified (Safeguarding relationships, interaction)

Dignified............................Standards

Productive (Safeguarding ideals promotion of: procreation, individual proficiency, profession)

Productive----------------------------Career

Civilized (Providing a supportive infrastructural means aligned to ideology)

Civilized............................Facilitation

Truthful (Accuracy of depiction, accumulation of knowledge)

Truthful...............................Archives

(Regional)----------------------------(Connected)

Faithful (Affirmation of understanding / enhancement of sensual- emotional self-actualization)

Faithful..............................Pledges

(Custom)----------------------------(Complete)

Wholesome Systematic values promoting integrated functionality

Wholesome...........................Secured

(System)..(Securities)

Ideal---Destiny

Faith…………………………………………………………….Natural Intelligence

Civics…………………………………………………………….Steller

Political----------------------------------- Wilderness Adaptive

Integrity--Judgement-Core

Such as:　　　　Doing/Being

　　　　　　　　Practice/Guidance　　　*As intelligence administration/formation: Guidance as doing

　　　　　　　　　　　　　　　　　　　*Therefor as complete/core: Guidance as being

Practical – Communal (Day to Day)	Guiding - Eternal (Forever, Always)	
Doing	**Being**	
Social Clubs	Inclusion and civics assignment/operations	
Conceptual configurations	Traditions building and overall configurations selection	
Universality	Doing and Being	and doing
Conformity and scale	Compatibility mechanized and scale relevancy	
Hierarchy and glorification	Function based class and admiration/cultivation	
Individuality and destiny	Practice and guidance	and practice
Destiny and Divinity	Direction and status	
Updating, merger	Popular and adaptive	
Abstraction and reason	Formulation and purpose	
Duality and mutual-reinforcement	Considerate and expanding interested	
Gender	Masculine, Feminine, Objective	

Being Judaic, as technological application of faith, as having judgement-core

Doing Judaic, as involving self into technological continuity, remaining within the image of intelligence able to preserve network status/reasoning/appreciation

Being Systematic Faith, as universal to all faith bound, pledged into the All Mighty
Doing systematic Faith, as complete systems of inner compatibility, of formal specialization and function-based access and privilege abridging ideals of integrity

Being healthy/conservative: As guiding reasonable in terms of inner intellectual design onto outwards will as per referenced and resource (access, privilege relevant)

Doing health/conservative lifestyles: Facilitating as adaptive/steadfast individuals, adaptive/function-premise family, governance adaptive/stable policies, faith as long term/networked cultivation

Being/Doing systematic Order: Establishing ideals in projection of a uniting destiny whose measure is an example/model as integrity. The civics, political adaptive towards the universally stabilizing integrity as ideal. Thereby, integrity is set as primary in being, and in doing the political/civics is short term adaptive as enhancing modifier.

Metaphors as mirrored, inversion, rotating, revolving: **Dynamic with a Core.**

Being/Doing Functional:

As enhancing, the modifications are **artistic**, layered to enable insights yet in relation to a premise being proposed.

As enhancing, the **developments** (modification) are examples of worship, words as instigating the actions in accordance to a pre-existing judgement foundation/core.

As enhancing, the **conditioning** (modifications) to social interaction safeguard the formalities binding relationships whose quality is measurable by the durability of those (binding) agreements

As enhancing, **procreation** (modification) expands and secures resources for access and privilege, such as from biological advancement of predispositions, cultivation of talent, and/or overall reward from professionalism

As enhancing, **support** (modification) enables **artistry, development, conditioning**, and **procreation**, to be livable in terms of ideals of integrity as instated knowledge, known and accepted.

As enhancing, **censorship** removes corrosive elements, invasive personas against the collective importance of knowledge, removing those against an integrity basis for the determination of judgement, refinement, or as consequence to actions to instill an enhancing feature to modifications.

As enhancing, **culturing** modification is an equation of understanding/refinement, **in relevancy to support and censorship**, enabling the dexterity of using both contents towards media for understanding and categorizing depictions into controllable, emotionally driven production

Wholesome as conclusions from enhancing and modifying, updated as establishing within a continuity of/as affirmation

Being: Citizen

Doing: Patriotic

Functional   **Individual** as Freedom to Specialize

Social as Liberty to acquire capitalist gain

        Individual & Social as facilitated by system

The measure of (civic/civil) goodness (functional/functioning) to bad (dysfunctional/malfunctioning)

As in relation to context: **formulated in determination of individual in relation to society**

As mandate (written accord signed into guidance over/as the representatives of people within the nation(s). These measures (definitions being detailed) are set as default, are taught as fundamentals, fundamental knowledge on how individuals specialize/operate and societies interpret/operate.

Fundamental: Gaining is safeguarded, durable as secured. Liberty is securement of freedom.

Thereby, freedom endures as liberty, enabling status, interconnecting perspectives, promoting culture as enhancing and naturally enables/promotes durable, beyond the baseline that is survival. Meaning brute strength is compartmentalized, as is intellectual pursuits as both are specialized, and together as collective attributes to conditioning: as per custom regional.

Civics Ideal
Functional Cultivation: Through Doing and Being

Doing (Accumulative to the status of being)

System Defaults...Experimental

Focus...Conclusive

Structured...Adaptive

*Variance within doing as using precedence, or formulating new combinations

Being (Relevant within functional determinations of doing

Wholesome as Upgrading

Clarity in relation to remaining precise

*Layered consideration within being as mindful in relation to bodily retention

Doing	Being
Promoting	Exemplifying

Can you do and be? Thereby inspiration/Inspirational

Civics Ideal in Participation to Technology

As ideal, within mechanical form, doing and being must compute/complete as functional.

The embedded configuration of an individual can be called a lifestyle, yet the specialized ability is in determination as willed, and in relevancy to resources and references.

Thereby, individuals institute mechanical form, as civilization, to enable, stabilize, and overall enhance resources and referenced, reinforcing the value, merit, obligations of determination/will.

As default, ideal, within mechanical form, doing and being must compute/complete as functional, meanwhile once stable the adaptive nature of expansion, experimentation requires formulated delicate safeguards towards innovations and self-interest.

*First the overall form is explained, and then by adding the feature that grows, the guidance matches the audience which are alive, as individuals as collectively.

Judgement-core Exemplified:

1 References considerations for Long-term as establishing securements

2 Resource considerations for Short term as adaptive, enhancing

3 System defaults long-term include leeway within being quality values establishes durability easement

4 Experimental short term segments emerge due to the adaptive living reactions therein

5 Intelligence Long-term safeguard categorization, responses securing vitals knowledge

6 Civics Short-Term enables collective choice, fortifies determination

7 Overall - The inner compatibility maintains in relation to an agreed upon structure of power, determination, adaptive as categorized into structured, diverse support

Determination-Core Exemplified

8 Inner to Overall as civics, this text, as converted for mechanical application to solidify the social diversity aspects in connectivity and compatibility to civics/civil structuring. 1-7 representing a brief of judgement-core contents, 8 representing a compliant civics determination core.

Objective Prioritization

Judgement-Core: Reference Permissions/Will

- **Premise to overall system (References)**
  - ○ Default mention of vital resources
- **Absolute Reference commands thus long term**

Premise Exemplified as/from Book 1-6 of Judgement Core

Determination-Core: Resource Data

- **Premise to market driven system (Resources)**
  - ○ Default mention of vital references
- **Absolute Resource commands thus short term (approved long term)**

Premise Exemplified as/from Book 1-7 of Judgement Core

Divinities-Core: Command/Mobilization Tactics

- **Premise to resource securement of references**
  - ○ Absolute Commands (thus securities and core culture)
- **Premise to reference securement of resources**
  - ○ Absolute Knowledge (thus core culture securities)

Premise Exemplified as/from Book 7 of Judgement Core

Objective Liberty

In terms of liberty, thereby judgement, determination and divinities are securements as functional status of an overall template securing a structure of power. The divinities is quoted as highest, yet bound to the principals of the judgement-core. Thereby, regardless how conflicting the communications, the default to is conform to integrity, which tends towards a peaceful, mindful interpretation of content/knowledge.

Individual/Social: Harmony as conclusive, as fulfillment

Civics: Order as Performance of Duty

Divinities: Doing and Being: Amen: Completion

Doing: Individual: Refreshed to engage

Doing: Social: Solutions Building/Engaging against oppression

Doing: Civics: Duty: Constrictive/Corrective

Doing: Divinities: Projecting Destiny

Being: Individual: Liberation refreshed

Being: Civics: Performance

Being: Social: Liberation to refresh

Being Divinities: Manifest Destiny

*Integrity Refreshing (Universal)

*Measurement: Resources/References: Judgement/Determination/Fulfilment of Will

*Custom regional as meaning arranging symbolic usage in adherence to liberty

Civic Arts

Refinement of Intellectualism

- Detailing of experimental, categorized as safeguarding

Refinement of Formal Knowledge

- Science as requiring instrumentation

Refinement as Hierarchies

- Industrial as mechanical application of formulated

Refinement as Creation

- Establishing Core
- Expansion

Civic Artistic Themes

- Deliberation
- Construction
- Organization

Civic Artistic Flavor

- Influence
- Encouragement
- Captivating/Focus/Convincing

Civic Artistic Compassion

- Achievement
- Discovery
- Meaning

Artistic Continuation

- Conforming to Integrity within Ranging subjects, themes
- Relevant to a localized region
- Destination Tourism

Artistic Accreditation/Privilege/Markets-Valued (Delicate)

- Stimulation (Sense of Appeal)
- Interpretation
- Condition
- Sensual
- Nationalism (Authoritative)
- Recognized, Structural Power
- Models

Artistic Control of Access

- Age
- Licensed Restrictions
- Maturity
- Authoritative Restrictions
- Education (Comprehension)

Artistic Censor/Edification into Satire or Rendered Exemplified

Unimportance…………………………Importance
Unwarranted Opinions……………Qualified Stance
Before Freedom………………………After Freedom
Before Liberty…………………………After Liberty
Criminal Intent………………………..Civil Liberty

Criminal Abuse…………………………Civil Discussion

*Experience or Sensibility: media category and maturity rating

Artistic Safeguards

If you want controversial media approved, revise satirical consideration, maintain integrity guidance

*Guidance set in differing eras, or otherwise tested within the extreme, may require fiction status/genre

Intellectual ability of audiences has been safeguarded or tested, or technically downgraded

* Media category and maturity rating

Careful authoritative designs, blatant misuse of concept, imitation of authoritative dystopia
* Media category and maturity rating

Social programs to enable content formation

* Media category and maturity rating

Civics Academia

As pro civics, advanced intellectual arts as liberal, and science with clear funding sources, both with premise:

Categorizes relevant to funding as

Cultural Relevancy (Liberal Arts as guidance, explanations)

- Archives proving civilization
- Political proving short term
- System displaying active model and normalcy (custom regional)
- Experimental exemplifying pivotal (propose pivotal as performance)
- Empirical intelligence such as automated intelligence, designing
- Civics configurations as organized social functions
- Steller

Scientific Relevancy

Structural Powers

- 1 Media
- 2 Education (Regulating Knowledge)

...

- 1 Justice
- 2 Military

...

- 1 Production
- 2 Government

...

- 1 Civics
- 2 Faith

It could be reasoned, that from refining observation, that we may observe the structural powers as having two levels of existence, in which they relate more directly, yet as vitals are integrated require each other as a thereby structure of power.

Notice 1 is the experimental and in that manner originator of 2

Notice 2 is the source as having priorities over 1, such as within developing from freedom to securements of liberty

Notice 2 are each long term, in relation to 1

Notice 2 are more difficult to alter altogether, require more paperwork, policy, adherences, than 1

*stable/experimental of 1 is from public feedback, causing 2 to be a naturally safeguarding organization, order of operations. (Relative to the scheduling, timed nature of content)

With feedback pivotal to all levels/layers of the proposed structure of powers, safeguarding the sensibility of public conformity, conditioning of sensitivity, reinforces each area of the structural powers is essential to the overall social validity constructed, and thereby abridging judgement, determination, onto stellar in cultural relevance/affirmation of destiny.

As ideal, civics is configured to enable experience, enable measure into determination which as emotionally driven, is enabled by priorities culturing/conditioning, such as in relation to **cultural relevance** and **scientific relevancy**. Thereof, faith is included, such as faith derived the formulation enabling civics as a judgement binding to validate determination, and determination requiring judgement as foundation, intellectual support structured.

Faith was used to originate formulation found in this text as civics considerations, as industry relevant conceptual, and thereby required bound within the formulation as both conclusion to judgement and determination, and in relation to validations of own foundation/founding-purpose.

Civics Determination of Faith

- Comprehension, objective as in determination of fundamental judgement values
  - As custom regional, adhering formal doctrines of established cultural and scientific relevancy (realistic, affirming leeway of connectivity)
- Adaptive as within framework meant across vast amounts of time
- Worship as means for citizenry to explore, intentions as safe kept in consideration of integrity as judgement formula
- Conservative as civics reinforcement of faith, such as within recycling,
- Commutability of faith, as in complex, layered and similarity towards biology and technology

Civics Determination of Conservative
(Default Civics as Pro Faith Defence)

Civics Determination of Conservative, ideally, as a demonstration that governance cares about resources. Default Civics as Pro Faith Defence as an abridgement between government and production is that of an abridgement of faith and civics, and further as promoted through media and education, defended by justice and militants, as an overall systemic, layered approach of self-determination, held/strengthened by a conceptual core as indoctrinated.

With Acari as a civics means to securement, thereby data storage as sacred, keeps backups and operational knowledge concerning vitals used for, across structural powers:

- Citizen ID
- Licensing Information/Registration
- Formalities of facilities
- Securements relating to physical materials, processing, storage standards
- Service descriptions and operational detail relating/promoting to increasing durability
- Arts, science and/as luxury details, such as in models developed/stored, custom regional arrangements relating to satisfying positions of authority

The technological pursuit of Acari systems, as the civics physical embodiment to this text, is that of enabling freedoms for operation in standard, relevant to technologies domestic in anticipation/direction to mobilization stellar: Yawaeh Systems.

Safeguarding of resource extraction itself, as well as methods and operational details, varies across many industries, such as onto tourism where the focus is directly upon experiences of an emotional arrangement, and either way, esteemed fashionable (assumed).

The predictably technological application, is to fabricate, maintain the environmental conditions in a manner where resources earned and resources used are calculated, yet the operational methodology are possibly highly valuable, such as for stellar performance. As (relatively) easy means to measure complex, and layered formations of operational undertaking.

*The default judgement-core reasoning, is that the projects remain within standards of health, with consideration as a system, that differing levels of potency render thus relative, the guidance thereof/therein provided.

Determination as civics focus on specialized pursuits/Interests

- Specialist industrial development as civics secured activities encouraging physical, intellectual labors
- Family cultivation of individual formations as encouraging physical, intellectual labors
- Tourism, service industries as providing/specialized in retrieve
- Custom reginal sensuality dedication as stability through organization, experimental
    - Contracting intellectual, physical secured judgment, as well as securing in terms of registration of facilitation of intellectual, physical secured determination

Determination as Civics Professions

- Resources reminder from civics that citizens do more than preform functions, they are cultivated and conditioning into layers of awareness, fulfillment, and encouraged into satisfaction
- Securing layers of industrial knowledge, livelihood across transformative upgrades to the infrastructure, especially within upgrading vitals
    - Upgrading the baseline defaults by providing options to work into, towards legacy (founding personas) figures
    - Being mindful other regions of the world require transitions of progress that require large scale development layers of reinforcing, supportive construction such as adapted to their regional resources as custom-rendering

Determination as State Configurations

- Creating short term political activation sequences where collective development plans attached to political motto being elected, enable democratic determination
- Reinforcement that survival of the technologically proficient requires a default amount of resources that as set within defaults of configuration, are elevated within the satisfactions of liberty, in which the political promise to prioritize emerging developmental cycles in conformity to an organized, coherent, compatible as reasonable.
- Voicing affirmations (requirements) in relation to reason and integrity (judgment) as to demand, vote into action determination towards extreme
- Status of leading within a multinational arrangement, reinforces technological vitals as at emergency level in relation to non-leading nations, whom may by contrast have lax views, considerations, and thereby can, should be approached with long term power-resource plans for the ameliorations enabling stellar conformities of a nevertheless centralized within civics arrangements.
    - Meaning trying to develop other regions into the leading nation's current conformity, is not possible (predictably), by the time the projects are built, the lead is already onto new generations of versions of adaptability, such as from diversified operations enhancing.
        - If the outwards development is not an enhancing feature, then such as through political, yet secured by state configuration, expansion is slowed or blacked until compatibility is restored/established

-

-

Civics Determination as State Configurations

Integration vs. Edification

- General requirements to older doctrines be adhered to, with integrity doctrines as lead filtering potential, such as by introducing ne layers of structural power to finally organized, process and operate all kinds of task and performance requirements their old paperwork cannot comply with
- Civics censorship defaults as art over graffiti, pro nationalism as structural powers allocated default gaming, media,
- Inner structural powers reserved usage, such as bound by formalities therein, exemplifying operational standards, offering collective insights, favoring appeals to civics determination
- Determination of civics as attempted beyond judgement, meaning judgement is adhered to, and projected destinations, destiny as long term and short term evaluated through enhanced performance

Civics Determination as Culture

- Technological pursuit as the esteem to what liberty is, as defining cultural perspective
    - Integrity bound as ecologically bound/sound
- Forging trade policy, as well as corporate and business incentives along projected and fulfilled traditions building to enhance domestic as capital technical lead interest
- Media driven as promoting essential to life, liberty resolutions
- Securities as positive affirmation of technological pursuit, a structural powers overall esteem towards a balance between/among encoding/encryption, and formalities, premise
- Securing context for the enabling of contractual formalities, such as enabling capital areas, exposition sites, networking displays as heritage areas, including centralizing areas into touristic and educational sites (or otherwise themed by structural powers and cultural relevancy) to a designated area, while working with, such as modify (as to adapt) existing surface areas to maintain or transfer commerce across/along considerations of capped market values
    - Change of fabrics and redevelopment into much larger areas, as meaning relative size and importance equates substantial move (potential state moving benefit for mass development as well as buy in features for local cultural assets/productions)
- Fixing celebrations to specific building locations, projects, including scale(occupancy size) of overall area (declaring movable festivities)

Civics Determination as Upgrading

- Upgrading as feedback relevant to wellbeing, as indicator of domestic peace
    - Equities leeway as developing what persona exemplifying trends
    - Requesting contextual information in reports, or noteworthy forwarded

Capital/Social   **Civics**

Domestic

Value/Demand   Establishes Reserves

Ownership Priced/Size   Survival Price Established

Luxury Price/Function   Industrial Priority Established

International-Empiric

    Commodity/Demand   Exchange Reserves

    Production/Capability   Development Potential

    Luxury/Trade Leeway   Reserves Potential

Steller

Steller/Mobilization   Civics Ready

Fundamental Determination as Integrity Formulation

Conceptual Core (Premise Foundation)

Long-term Stability – Civics- Faith Reserves

Being Healthy determined as Integrity Ideals, a Systematic Approach, as meaning a framework of ideas centralized as functional in termination of overall fulfillment of categories, as it's conclusive upgrading, upkeep as the wholesome feature: The ideal framework of health as systematic awareness, as conceptual, systems basis to judgement-core.

Doing Health as (Contextually Driven)

Short Term Adaptive – Politically Driven/Applicable

Doing Healthy Determination as

- Promoting Individual and social boundaries

- Enhancing field beauty, actively within state configuration

- Esteems on fulfillment of relationship standards

- Cultivating through infrastructure as civics matter

- Faithful as samples, example, and models used within securement of healthy determination

- Safekeeping production vitals in functioning of enhancement features cultured

- Maintaining wholesome as upgrading as arising, mindful of stellar as destiny in design, conformity compute, conclude/abridge

*Individuals as in formation to lifestyles, and their relevance and in conforming to each other (civics usage, the admiration of examples as confirming to layered supports approach

* Segmented as options, elections relevant

Civics Integrity

Conclusive, Collective-Configuration/Embodiment

As universally applied/applicable, Integrity has several formation/formula. As universal, its (Integrity) ability to exist and be relevant across all judgement subject matter as a stable reference guiding measure/operations-design, then an overall configuration of, for being and doing necessitates this doctrine as covering the resources section, indicating a fortification of will version called divinities core..

Examining Integrity Formula as applicable in layers (social: judgement core, Civics: determination core, Divinity: Command, mobilization).

Healthy

Socially: That Health as fundamental extends into the significant of all ideals

Civics-Civil: That health as a leading component of judgement, applies onto all civics matters as measurable

Divine: That health has been identified as of core important to the meaning of all things/life

Beautiful

Socially: Centered on terms of health, the individuality of health reflects variance projected

Civics-Civil: That beauty relates to judgement, and is nevertheless function based literal

Divine: That the importance of beauty endures, onto, as everlasting

Loving

Socially: Interweaves judgement aspects of resource, references and determination of will core to expansion

Civics-Civil: In determination of long term self and collective cultivation plans

Divine: Enhancing depictions promoting the mobilization of virtue

Dignified

Socially: In determination of long term self and collective cultivation plans

Civics-Civil: Functions orientated as in relation to larger production formations

Divine: Enabling of automated intelligence within the formation of civics and infrastructure itself

Productive

Socially: The enabler of overall civilization as grouping of completed systems united/uniting

Civics-Civil: The facilitation of both stability and enhancing experiential

Divine: The emergence of core towards the restoration, establishing of God's direction

Faithful

Social: Long term bounds, in edification of transitional

Civics-Civil: Long term bound, displayed as short term abridgement to custom regional

Divine: An overall model, sample establishing direction

Truthful

Socially: Point of intellectual, policy maturation, status of references

Civics-Civil: Point of physical in addition to default intellectual, policy maturation, status of references

Divine: Command and mobilization as cultural, mechanically applied (universal defaults)

Wholesome

Socially: Wellbeing and in respects to upgrading

Civics-Civil: Wellbeing embedded into the default of structuring and its intelligence/perspective

Divine: A collectors of completed fulfillments, of compartmentalized adaptive

Socially: That Health as fundamental extends into the significant of all ideals

Civics-Civil: That health as a leading component of judgement, applies onto all civics matters as measurable, involved as survival reserves and collective across systems offering prosperity defaults

Divine: That health has been identified as of core important to the meaning of all things/life

...

Civics **Healthy** as a conclusive formula for Judgement Core (Rising as collective in comprehension approved)

As healthy relates to enabling the body to function

Civics Defaults:

Public health as most reasoning to safeguard the largest amount of bodies, displayed as per likely positive-influence for targeted age/maturity groups

- Especially obvious to segments where reduction lowers grievances
- Promoting the style as common themed actions found generally beneficial
- Contextual as focusing on participation of interest
    - Cultivation: Promoting known calibrations to be fruitful/productive
    - Nurture default: Fuels of Resources, also in relation to maintain
    - Defensive allocation: assuring longevity
    - Injured status as necessarily assumed not knowing what is needed, as to be tended to not guided
    - Injury as disruption meaning there is a need to reform as to not compromise
- The observation of context, also in relation to holdings secured, to regional academia, and structural powers recommendations/allowances
    - In network of sampler, observation tools
    - Devices to enable system to respond, dedicated maintainers of sensory additions, enhancers (possible Archives relevancy)
- Exploring taste, enjoyment of tastes as sanctioned, feedback setups
    - General food and environmental monitoring through regional sampling based on large volumes of usage
    - As good taste, a sense of being alive in the supportive across various levels of operations offering fulfillment
        - Imagery in relation to attributing, as raising esteems of themes building reference
        - Poetic adherence, formalities of intellectual or contextual symbolism
            - Potential need to justify interpretation in relation to records

Civics Defaults – Memory Storage

Healthy as Memory

Memory with added self-status is embedded, an experience with emotion as result to signal, such as from detachment (similar to adding light display when operational)

- Topic of display memory signaled upon unplug
- Symbols priority remembering, brands/registered class as included potentially in added
- Per structured power as governance-fields/property districts, usage
- Network capability as to endure/execute as send only, secured recovery (library default)
- Layers of access each with backup into achieving next area, if common room placed
    - Frequencies
    - Power, reserves status

Healthy as Memory

Formulated into Esteems

Civics locked into services

Political mass usage of resource, heritage engineering

Databases:

- Complete status as Knowledgeable
- Display status as operational

In Field Support:

- Model examples/forms
- Policy, reference access
- Civics & Faith Defaults
    - Differing categories of traditions (access, privilege) forging
    - United in the relevance
    - Wholesome as contained, and thereof upgrade

*In consideration of Data, such as from Integrity Matrix

Integrity Matrix Data Template
Truth as Data Central

Healthy (Functional body) -

*Truth as bodily configurations, such as to bypass, technological as ecology benefits

Beauty (Functional deciphering of sensual stimuli)

*Truth as organs reactions specific, sensibility repeating model cycles

Loving (Functional emotion reaction in relation to situation / circumstance, safeguarding expression / actions)

*Truth as layered in particular of previous, concludes and strategic formations

Dignified (Functional relationships, safeguarding interaction)

*Truth as signed up for, as specifically agreed upon, formation of relationship premise

Civilization (Providing a supportive infrastructure, direction, maintenance, safeguarding individuals /society)

*Truth as citizen, with opportunities to excel/advance or rise as acceleration, of membership, in relation to access, esteem and privileges

Faith (Affirmation of understanding / enhancement of sensual- emotional self-actualization)

*Truth as guidance, with a forward, accuracy able to exemplify predictions

Productive – Functional lifestyles, from profession to procreation (Safeguarding long-term traditions of talent, and biological continuation)

* Truth as mentionable, strategic evaluations talent

Wholesome as Upgrading be default of maintaining, adjusting, formations

*Truth as applicable, mentioned as guidance poetic, or otherwise conclusive on common clarifications (predictably advised)

Truth as then explaining, to fill in the following:

Archives - Explanations of physical components to health

System - Body as Having Physical Intelligence and Intellectual: **configurations**

Supreme - Layered Healthy (**formulas** based from system observations/awareness)

Stellar – As the potency of **faith, biology, technology** enable

Consider the infrastructure remains, enact as functional/functioning

- Service detail - To remain stocked and prepared, or pending (secured as potency adjustable)
- Service functioning, powered, maintained
- Constituted for the environment conditioned into/for/motivational

Adjustment of service detail and center of functioning, as themed, contracted

Infrastructural Vitals

- Festive areas as huge stimulants for the look, arrangement, preparations across the landscape
    o Per structural power as infrastructural dominance

Civics Ideals - Beautiful as Retrieve
Rejuvenate Through Services

- Resting options to replenish strength
- Coordination to reinforcing events
- Raising quality of sleep (noise reduction)
- Pro diets, purposeful meal combinations
- Soothing aches, influencing moods
- Deprive/reform focus potential as restore premise purpose, maintain core considerations
    o Highlight or untangle clutter, refocus as better angle of entry/identification
- Recreation and personal time as having options organized from civics, maintaining individual quality, maintaining regional conformities, maintaining as civics feature
- Reflecting on the brain as fragments and as whole, from inner experiences, to ideas generated within layers therein experienced further,
- Dreams, and dreams interpretation, inspirational
    o Movement theorems, sensory experiences
- Self-refinement Intellectual, emotional, component/technologies driven
- Conditioning projects
- General leeway towards creation,
- Culture centre promoting societal aspects (active, current parts of heritage)

*Removing dystopia projections displayed, exemplified, protecting general public interest

Civics Ideals - Loving as Careful
Well Being Through Cheerful

- Responses as in the positive, as in reinforcement of formalities of loving commitments, and their particular arrangements,
- Response leeway enabled from the formalities received, presented, and the approach positive to those statements as freedoms of speech, freedom of being, and freedom of privacy,, in a complex and layered consideration
- Careful selection in relation to solutions building, solutions providing as themselves in relation to public allowances, such as versus privet conversations

Healthy Prioritization (Functional bodies relating)

*Priorities as bodily configurations, such as to bypass, technological as ecology benefits

Beauty (Functional deciphering of sensual stimuli)

* Priority as organs reactions specific, sensibility repeating model cycles

Loving (Functional emotion reaction in relation to situation / circumstance, safeguarding expression / actions)

* Priority as layered in particular of previous, concludes and strategic formations

Dignified (Functional relationships, safeguarding interaction)

* Stimulation/dedication as signed up for, as specifically agreed upon, formation of relationship premise

Civilization (Providing a supportive infrastructure, direction, maintenance, safeguarding individuals /society)

* Priority as citizen, with opportunities to excel/advance or rise as acceleration, of membership, in relation to access, esteem and privileges

Faith (Affirmation of understanding / enhancement of sensual- emotional self-actualization)

* Priority as guidance, with a forward, accuracy able to exemplify predictions

Productive – Functional lifestyles, from profession to procreation (Safeguarding long-term traditions of talent, and biological continuation)

* Priority as mentionable, strategic evaluations talent

Wholesome as Upgrading be default of maintaining, adjusting, formations

* Priority as applicable, mentioned as guidance poetic, or otherwise conclusive on common clarifications (predictably advised)

Civics Ideals - Loving as Careful
Loving Through Rejuvenation

- Learning regulation into experiences, as having to strengthen vigor, as character formation in relevancy of conditioning (typical standard)
- A default of logics, judgement as perhaps vague compared to determination, yet clear in the direction overall of premise vs. of focus derived assumed soundly
- Culturing loving as relating to priorities, and of respecting the prioritization between people to forge dignified relationships
- Social, cultural recollection as experiences bound, shared, active culture as remembered vital heritage points
- Determination as deciphered, whereas judgement guides values, determination as structured, already involving systems implemented, operations of valued united
  - Loving assumes completed, formal systems assigned memberships are valid
- The needs of determination already involving matured states of input, contribution, civics as already established resources, references, and as testament in virtue of will sanctified (long term adhered)
- Whereas judgement-core is about precedence building precedence, Acari as determination core is about bound, social into civics cultured networks implemented into operating,
  - A functional model in design as nevertheless sound in judgement
- The promotion of production as physical manifestation of judgement, celebrated as civics as bound to reserves, as relevant to secured factors themselves considered into involvement/cheer
- Encouraging the deciphering of systems in explainable, established recognition having sensibilities added as devices are guided sound in template.
  - Whereas template enable variance made compatible, having options as relevant to custom regional resources, references, and will as terms or ease of usage in relation to structured powers (predictably)
- Freedom of speech within civics, as membership privilege, access within formalities mentioned, stated as chosen regulation, as means to control and therein assumed to refine
- Intellectual concerns as educational or be default assigned by stature powers
- Emotional conditioning as regional custom, yet media exemplified as emergency examples/considerations required (establishing reason, through media applied)
- Determination as buildings solutions, purpose of specific buildings initiated as collaborations, enablers

Civics Ideals - Loving as Careful
Survival-Defaults - Reactive

- Public calm despite anger: Determination to rid of a disruption, leeway in accordance to negative guidance, or in disregard from arrangement/behaviour, context is public policy guiding is not being adhered
- Stupidity found, as multiple testing of same or general conditions, of which the testing itself is not permitted, been provide and accepted as wrong on terms of previous warnings
- Increase in public measure in determination the actions found are part of patterns of action which conflict against an individual and social policy.
    - Discard that the mobilization to monitor or intervene isn't itself an infraction. Yet as relevant to formalities, possibly resourced and referenced as multinational intrusive
- Total removal as in determination of infrastructural defences, obvious mobilization, permissions
- Memorial sites as in relevance to strategic considerations of networked infrastructural defence
- Media depiction of large scale refugee, and other mass relocations relevant
- Heritage as needful considerations, active operations acknowledgement
- Heritage as in esteem to principals, criteria orientated
- Displays of public character, forms to use

Civics Ideals - Loving as Careful
Quality of Life – Reactive

- Resolutions reactions as in measure of functional and durability
    - Functional as not requesting, undertaking as responsive
    - Durable as not in distress

*Resolving as a defensive and nurturing conclusions rendering

*Spiritual as in influence of others as collective grace, of mindful, collective

System determination as pledges, assumes nevertheless an accuracy in formalities

Civics Ideals – Dignified as Fulfilling

Quality of Life – Reactive

Dignified as integrity layered into conditions accepted, developing of fulfillment, and satisfaction values for life. As structural powers, or cultural and scientifically relevant, the fulfillment is relevant to differing placed, placement values assumed for, towards attaining refinement for specialized interest rendering (resources, references, determination of will (specific/specialist)

Healthy Stimulation/dedication (Functional bodies relating) -

*Stimulation/dedication as bodily configurations, such as to bypass, technological as ecology benefits

Beauty (Functional deciphering of sensual stimuli)

* Stimulation/dedication as organs reactions specific, sensibility repeating model cycles

Loving (Functional emotion reaction in relation to situation / circumstance, safeguarding expression / actions)

* Stimulation/dedication as layered in particular of previous, concludes and strategic formations

Dignified (Functional relationships, safeguarding interaction)

* Stimulation/dedication as signed up for, as specifically agreed upon, formation of relationship premise

Civilization (Providing a supportive infrastructure, direction, maintenance, safeguarding individuals /society)

* Stimulation/dedication as citizen, with opportunities to excel/advance or rise as acceleration, of membership, in relation to access, esteem and privileges

Faith (Affirmation of understanding / enhancement of sensual- emotional self-actualization)

* Stimulation/dedication as guidance, with a forward, accuracy able to exemplify predictions

Productive – Functional lifestyles, from profession to procreation (Safeguarding long-term traditions of talent, and biological continuation)

* Stimulation/dedication as mentionable, strategic evaluations talent

Wholesome as Upgrading be default of maintaining, adjusting, formations

* Stimulation/dedication as applicable, mentioned as guidance poetic, or otherwise conclusive on common clarifications (predictably advised)

Stimulation/dedication as then explained to fill in the following:

Archives - Explanations of physical components to health

System - Body as Having Physical Intelligence and Intellectual: **configurations**

Supreme - Layered Healthy (**formulas** based from system observations/awareness)

Stellar – As the potency of **faith, biology, technology** enable

Civilized

Civilized as configuration in facilitation, regional infrastructure potential, what does your membership in one area or another imply

Civilization (Providing a supportive infrastructure, direction, maintenance, safeguarding individuals /society)

Healthy Civilized: Artistry **(Functional pro infrastructural as body)**
* **Artistry** as bodily configurations, such as to bypass, technological as ecology benefits

Beauty (Functional deciphering of sensual stimuli)

* **Artistry** as performance specific, sensibility repeating titles profiled

Loving (Functional emotion reaction in relation to situation / circumstance, safeguarding expression / actions)

*Truth as layered in particular of previous, concludes and strategic formations

Dignified (Functional relationships, safeguarding interaction)

* **Artistry** as signed up for, as specifically agreed upon, formation of relationship premise

Civilization (Providing a supportive infrastructure, direction, maintenance, safeguarding individuals /society)

Artistry as citizen, with opportunities to excel/advance or rise as acceleration, of membership, in relation to access, esteem and privileges

Faith (Affirmation of understanding / enhancement of sensual- emotional self-actualization)

* **Artistry** as guidance, with a forward, accuracy able to exemplify predictions

Productive – Functional lifestyles, from profession to procreation (Safeguarding long-term traditions of talent, and biological continuation)

* **Artistry** as mentionable, strategic evaluations talent

Wholesome as Upgrading be default of maintaining, adjusting, formations

* **Artistry** as applicable, mentioned as guidance poetic, or otherwise conclusive on common clarifications (predictably advised)

Artistry as then explaining, to fill in the following:

Archives - Explanations of physical components to health

System - Body as Having Physical Intelligence and Intellectual: **configurations**

Supreme - Layered Healthy (**formulas** based from system observations/awareness)

Stellar – As the potency of **faith, biology, technology** enable

Faithful as symbolic embodiment, of universal appeal, or regional reinforcement as a collective whim

Truthful as Passion

Destiny as Objectivity
Truth as a Civics ideal, has layers of recognition.

Archives

- Truth as guidance
- Truth as direction, such as experimental guidance

System

- Truth as System directions
- Truth as trends, and emerging innovative

Administrative within system

- Truth as intelligence configuration
- Truth as civics compatibility and user connectivity

Research and Development (long term trajectory therein)

- Truth as destiny, stellar

...

The truth as having multiple layers of function or priority within judgement-core, as enabling compartmentalization into specialist reinforced as design to system stability, and adaptor with advancing experimental

In relation to guidance, differing subject matters and means to approaching, introducing, using the knowledge, means help is complex, such as to convert and condition long term or to answer questions such conversation or conditioning enables as every day specialist ability/talent/profession?

Era as contextually driven knowledge, as requiring the answering system to hold all the answers as key or insight, yet to what invested interest is there in examination, or approval. What is the mutual trajectory forward?

Truth as mentioned in this text, if universal attributes to ideals, thus useful in focusing determination:

Quality

Artistry

Productive as integrity in relation to cultivating professional whim and passion with recreational reinforce, long term resource chosen support to enhance upgrade into

Wholesome as upgrading, in connectivity to refining pursuits, of templates, on premise designs both of being whole in relation to, and of knowing the enhancement features of compartmentalized adaptive

Properties found as stable/part of Ideals as archives, and so the results as integrating into system awareness:

(Overall Conceptually-Fulfilling (Indicator) Attributes Found within/with Ideals)

Durability……………………………………… (Health)

Satisfaction…………………………………….(Beautiful)

Artistry (Science defaults) ………………..(Civilization)

Stimulation/dedication ……………………(Dignified-Relationships)

*Procreation as Universal Adaptive Pending

Esteem/Configurations………………………(Production)

Priority/bound……………………………… (Loving)

Whole/enhancing…………………………….(Faithful)

Upgrade/settings……………………………..(Wholesome)

	Judaic Soul	
Reincarnation	Incarnation	Reformation
Reason	Refinement	Strategy
Reference	Resource	Will
Social	Civics	Divinities

Civics Conditioning Amenities / Venue Selection

- Mental Preparation

    o Symbols exemplifying understanding
    o Conceptual diagrams (as book, program fragments)

Civics System Components

Pleasantries Sample

In the beginning there was desire for things, and they themselves began

Time as forming thicker, or being consumed such as with heat and (and from being in relation to another) force

The kindness felt at home, generally in arrangement to that regions formality using faith and that or those individuals entertaining/entertained

Rising voices of upgrade, the receipt onto inventory selections, of gifts in recollection

Rendering sacred names honored, in poetic across Medias of expression

-    Ceremonies were the material fabric I he ash absorbed into the skin is pleasant, welcome, useful
In the broadcast of echo, as in network, of communications (as an instillation, as a sanctuary, indicator)

-    Sorting about deciphering, the distinguishing of/between, as the comparative using a measure. Establishing measures as the context of the premise, or in the principal detail, were limitations old
-    Mapping as into display, schedules, as to personify sound (themed music accord, networked as per selection (: co dependant ID and affirmation conclusion)

Reservations as Sanctuary for Members/Animals (dedicated sites)

Criteria for admission/entrance/membership

-    Based on overall age reached
-    Areas dedicated to flying animals
-    Areas dedicated to ground animals
-    Areas with sea animals
-    A place for odd yet cute, cute as adorable or endearing
-    Fountains
-    Swimming areas
-    On site harvest, supplies cultivation
-    Strategic reasoning for placement:
-    Near council of regional power, to show compassion
-    As strategic do not pass, or guarded barrier
-    Seasonal Reserves, supplies (based on mass storage ease)

Supreme Structural Powers

Media-Civics Supreme default Examples (Focal points, production campaigns)

Justice: Live Duty

Military: Militia games

Media: Media Trivia

Education: Quiz Challenge

Government: Spotlight news

Faith: Biology, technology, faith

Civics: Configurations

Production: Products (and in relation to access from structural powers)

*Worthy as contextual to relevant power structure, training, traditions

*Having specific introductions made, such as in esteem to locations of heritage for the structure of power

*Access to stored inventory based on membership to supreme structure of power category/division

*Default gift or emergency allowance, such as transportation or refuge; with equipment or supply

*Emergency credit, emergency on site field work (potential priority on upper qualification)

*Emergency trade of comport or luxury, such as preapproved, as enabled in advance (options)

*Emergency trophies trade, selling, exchange (personal, formal collections)

Civic Default Public-Celebration Allocation - Ritual Traditions
- Wind as representing souls
- The star formation in relevance to the solar system and the galaxy as central focal point, of from the point of most illuminating in the sky appearing as background
- Power ritually symbolized by radiating light
- Victory celebration as feasting and drinking
- Tournament related marriage proposals. Announcements
- Celebrating house wives, victory moments (toasting, complimenting)
- Pilgrim's staff, walking cane, or other symbol to wear and have default, visitor approved status
- Crumpling of leaves, the spray of confetti, effects to announce end, completion, event focal point with time to otherwise depart
    - Package content

Burial Sites

- Visiting grounds
- Registration and visitation (Administrative network)
  - ID membership
  - 24 hour access potential
  - Tombs
  - Featured appearances (travel packages)
  - Eloquent paths
  - Minerals area, beauty pieces sold, sales allocation
  - Devices to monitor for mischief, cleverly installed, such as lodged in thick material

National Compatibility

- Use of ancient formality into agreed upon template adherence in all regions, whose formality enables the desire to preserve such as tradition, adding a culture of reinforced conditioning journeys
- God's favor, as in esteem to what premise, such as authored, such as of judgment core being a fulfillment in relation, in being ready validating the all mighty
- Development plans, in regards to multinational, binding accords (Empiric presence)
- Military celebrations in Spring
- An overall esteem to guide visitors well
- Sympathy towards national character, as in relevancy towards formal criteria and membership access
- A valid/default association of nationalism and flying

Hospital

- Equipment Specialties
- Supplies strategically enabled (area of fabrication, local materials supply)
- Nurse Core as knowledge Database (Archives)
- Doctors (travel benefit towards secured room, facilities)
- Network buy in plans, for travel and hospital needs combined
- Recovery Sites (duration vs. location requirements)
- Ventilation requirements
- Ventilation requirements specifically for transportation area
- Different body sized rooms, if applicable
  - Tools, equipment implications?

*Media must ask casual stories only (onsite)

Civic Landmark

Maintained vantage points, kindness in features

- For seeing far into the horizon
- Entry restrictions (weapons, armor)
- Experimental show/events site (assumed seasonal)
    - Speaker setup
- Picnicking, lounging structure
- Devices against air attacks
- Chorus Structure (acoustic site)
- Holiday themes (rotating as storage, decorations)
- Honoring of hero
- Favor/chivalry: experimental
- Poetic Site (with guided explanation)
- The (ideal) beauty of woman/women
- Offerings (nature, fertility), ecological goodness
- Defense from wildlife if observation point
- Parks dedicated to operational whereabouts for structural powers
- Placed in boundary to forge objective feedback
- Monitored site for pick up, send off (semi touristic, such as informational)
- License to play live music at landmark site (easements)
- Approved wisdoms, for quick landmark creation
- Caution sign for uneven ground, or for transportation
- Indications for transportation
- Maiden landmarks as, willing to premise, or exploring romantic dedication plans
- Artistic leeway as foolish or frantic, yet in depth explanation, such as in relevancy to slogan/motto and premise (vaguer than historic, potential part of a continuity to heritage)
- Hot watered sanitation as networked, developed
- Communications interactive (possibly/regional integrated into other networks of connectivity)
- Spectacle/Events area (designation)
- On site solar, wind or water current powered energy (or other renewable, resource)
- Network connectivity

Connection to emergencies broadcast system
Tracking of foreign ID, Touristic Highlights, packages resources reminders updates
Feedback

Civic Landmark – Historic

- Depicting earlier formation, details
- Explaining the development, progress
- Explaining relevant experimentation/discovery

Civic Landmark

- Signs for local resources, services
    - o Fuel
    - o Eating
    - o Supplies//Equipment
    - o Hospital
    - o Civics program
    - o Information
    - o Local Services
    - o Local Industries
    - o Route Indications
    - o Recovery area

Detection of status of neglect

- Wear and tear along routes
- Frequency-infrequency highlight/alert
- Detection/connection with sanctuary network, civics network
- Issue with limbs, pieces, parts (moving)
    - o Noise indicator

Shelters – Base/Mobile Emergency Solutions

- For people in shock
- For people injured
- For waiting injured for a duration (recovery timing)
- Grieving sites
- Mechanisms to lock and release packages
    - o Easement to reload, refresh stock

Emergency Communication Database/Network

Consent request – license easement

Accuser – assistance call

Explanations to emergency situations

Emergency Packages

- Announcements
- Vestments

Journey Packages

- Regional selections
- Themed production sampling
- Themed civics arrangement/activity
- Romance reserves, dedicated journeys
- Honeymoon

General Packages

Containment options and transportation thereof arranged

- Lost and found system of recovery
- Tools collection
- Historical information, journey, routes
  - Intended popular

Tourism - Supreme Structures
- Old Military Instillations, palaces
  - Dates

  - Cataloging outer styles of material, patterns (modern recreations, theme buildings)

    - Weathering process involved such a heat baked?

    - Layers to foundations in original (can materials be changed to augment)

    - Material mixes, new mixtures versus ancient, changes in durability

      - Cataloging surface textures

        - Smooth

        - Shiny

Tourism - Symbolic Regional Custom

Fabrics and material quality standards

- Wearable symbols (material usable on flesh, prolonged usage tested)

- Chains durable (no fashion only chain, safety bounds)

- Decorative light weight supplies for regional custom artistic fabrications

  - Beads

  - Local stones as small, portable objects

- Heavier stone or heavy materials for static emplacement

  - Vassals

- Largescale landscaping arrangements as indoors (protecting from erosion)

  - Use of mouldable supplies fabric for outdoor usage

- Non degrading metals for kitchen, eatery

- Nontoxic clays, materials for pottery

- Basic impact durability as hard, flexibility durability as soft fabric usable

    - Dishes

    - Reusable, daily vitals

    *Significant recycling, composting (sustainable) programs as enabling leeway

Tourism - Museums places

- As justifying production
- Offering volumes of insights, considerations

- Highlighting generosity of owners, regional powers, managers of note (noteworthy as exemplified)

- Academic explanations areas or overall themes if formality of title premise

- Domestic becomes international collections, potential formality of title premise

- Date, dimensions detailing if applicable

- First models, first mass scaled operations/fabrications

        - Differing materials used

- Limitations and expansion into new fabrics, materials used (assumed developmental explanations)

- Original purpose of location, building, equipment, supplies as developed/developing

- Custom arrangements to facilitate themselves sources of innovation, if applicable

        - Interesting requirements, technical requirements: audience expected, financing relevancy

- Original site plans, vs./and development look, feel, experiences

- General adaptations

- Relevant local discoveries

- Sample rooms, model representative areas

        - Depicting era

        - Depicting local origins in production relevancy (as proficient)

Tourism - Museums places - Authenticity ironies

- Erosive, corrosive materials no longer used do to danger, so re-usage for display as non-acceptable, not authentic as promoting production ideal

        - Alterations and reasoning included as conceptually driven, nor eroding experiences required

- Dealing with thieves, invasion

Themes of Focus - Filtering Content

Dynamic story telling formulas

- Mindful of exaggerations

    - Categorical as media fantasy-fiction or media historic

    - Puzzle formations mapped out

        - Criteria for unlocking through specific paths/avenues of transitions

- Outcome modified within selections chosen as adaptive/interactive components

- Creating solving mechanism, scenarios and answer to assemble into passages connecting options/decisions

- Decoding patterns, creating patterns unmasking trickery as learning themes or styles of designs

- Adapting volumes of storyline into premise formulations, such as transitions into new eras of learning/adaptation

- Establishing enjoyable reference points, highlighting known intrigues among volume selections/options rendering

- Compliance to formalities, such as touristic implementation

- Highlighting errors in instructions and results, casualties (through story telling)

- Exploring easily, or complex misleading

- Adventures of hope as attainable

- Exploring racial conditioning, highlights in differences: as highlighting specialized features

    - Potential re-examination of historical, past development to re-examine future developments predictable

- Exploring appearance stated versus experience driven

- Practical conditioning journeys

    - Academic

    - Discipline forging

    - Physical training

    - Talents and hobbies into membership and partition

- Exploring scope differences such as administrative along worker performance insights

    - Potential settings for viewer, user to participate with either, or both blended/contrasted

    - Language simplification/complexities

- Themed per structural power

- Detailing greatness or wonderment (fantasy enhanced)

- Explaining regulation as simplified and examples based

- Explaining historic territorial disputes

- Exploring eras of fashionable, establishing contextual

    - Contrasting

- Adapting to extreme conditionings, adapting to natural environments

- Cultivating the environment through technological purpose

- Fortune building

- Power management, models of might as influence rendering

    - Natural themes of magnitude as elite symbols reinforcing sceneries (assumed applicable)

- Exploring meanings as drought into illumination

- Faith dedications, long term dedication

    - Reinforcement through ritualized performance/depictions

- Reinforcing endurance principals/formulas for performance

- Examples of overcoming grief, establishing/re-establishing purpose

- Trance as poetic, artistic layering of senses, as sense of self overlapping story, abridging conclusions/depictions between being and doing

- Adaptive recovery

- Displaying quotes and passages into storyline lived through audience participation/contemplation